THIS BOOK IS DEDICATED TO MY WIFE
FRANCES

PREFACE

THIS new dictionary reflects the remarkable changes which have occurred in the advertising world in the last few years. A whole new jargon has emerged in the fields of agency, design, media and research, while certain aspects such as direct response marketing and sales promotion have developed new techniques and expanded. There have also been big changes in the law such as the Copyright, Designs and Patents Act, the Data Protection Act, and the Consumer Protection Act. A new edition of the British Code of Advertising Practice has been published.

Fleet Street has vanished, satellite TV has arrived, and conventional radio and TV are being revolutionised. From digital design to balance sheet brand valuations, it is an ever-changing new world. As far as possible at any point in time, this dictionary attempts to capture the language of this kaleidoscopic world of advertising.

I am grateful to those who have generously supplied information, and most sources are acknowledged in the references. I am also grateful to trade journals such as *Campaign*, *Direct Response Marketing*, *Marketing Week* and *Precision Marketing* which have kept me up-to-date.

With an increasing number of students preparing for BTEC, LCCI, CAM and CIM examinations, this book should be essential to their understanding of advertising. It will complement my three books in the M & E Handbook series.

This dictionary should also be enlightening to those who work in advertising, or in any business which uses advertising.

Croydon, February 1989.

A

à la carte agencies. Creative agencies which do no media buying and so do not need 'recognition' by the media owners' organisations. They can place ads through media independents, or clients can do so separately. Sometimes called 'second wave' agencies. *See* THIRD WAVE AGENCIES.

AA. *See* ADVERTISING ASSOCIATION.

A/B split method. Another name for split run media testing, a control and a test advertisement appearing in different editions of a journal on the same day and in the same position. Similarly, different advertisements can be exposed on different radio or TV stations or different transmitters of the same station. Response or recall can be measured to decide the most effective advertisement.

ABAA. *See* ASSOCIATION OF BUSINESS ADVERTISING AGENCIES.

ABMRC. Association of British Market Research Companies.

above-the-line advertising. Sometimes called media advertising. Relates to traditional commission paying media: press, TV, radio, cinema, outdoor. Media handled by full service agencies. *See* BELOW-THE-LINE.

ABSA. *See* ASSOCIATION FOR BUSINESS SPONSORSHIP OF THE ARTS.

accents, floating. *See* FLOATING ACCENTS.

account. An advertising agency or PR consultancy client.

account controller, executive, handler. A person who acts as liaison between an agency or consultancy and clients. Once known as 'contact man'. He presents client needs to the agency, proposals to the client, and generally maintains the agency-client relationship, supervising progress of a campaign.

account planner. In an advertising agency the person who

1

integrates the work of departments and personnel, planning a creative brief, and working closely with the ACCOUNT CONTROLLER. He is concerned with research, marketing, promotional strategy and the day-to-day direction of the campaign.

ACORN. A Classification of Residential Neighbourhoods market analysis which defines 36 types of census enumeration districts and classifies 12 housing groups, and 36 housing types. Can be applied to selective mailings or MAILDROPS aimed at residents of particular classes of housing. Created by CACI Market Analysis, London. *See also* MONICA, MOSAIC, PIN, SUPERPROFILES.

acronym. Short attractive name usually derived from the initial letters of a long business name, or a wordy description. For example, Fiat is derived from Fabbrica Italiana di Automobili Torino, meaning Italian car factory in Turin.

ad hoc **survey.** Single, one-off research survey, complete in itself, as distinct from a continuous research such as CONSUMER PANEL or DEALER AUDIT.

adaption. Variation of basic advertisement lay-out and copy to fit different spaces, shapes and sizes.

adequate distribution. Ensuring that stocks of a product are available in shops to meet demand created by advertising. It is necessary to co-ordinate selling-in and delivery to retailers.

Adline. Regional advertising and publicity magazine. Sponsors ROSES AWARD for creative work in the regions. Monthly, Birmingham, 1985.

Admap. Covers media, advertising research, marketing. Holds annual conference. Monthly, London, 1984.

Adshel superlite. A back-lit poster that performs best on dull days and at night. Supplied by More O'Ferrall.

Advans. 48-sheet, mobile, vertical two-sided advertisement that occupies an entire vehicle behind the driver's cab. Advans, London.

advertisement analysis. MEAL service giving description of every press and television advertisement placed during the month for each brand. Every advertisement is listed by date within brand and shows details of: date of appearance; TV station and channel or publication; spot length or size; time-on, special position, use of colour; rate card cost; whether it is a RANGE ADVERTISEMENT in which case the costs are divided equally between products in the range; whether it is a co-operative advertisement (in which case the total cost is given to the prime advertiser, and the secondary advertiser is listed); whether it is a Dealer advertisement (pre-fixed 'T'). Total expenditure and sub-totals for press and television are shown for each brand and the product group. *See* MEAL.

advertisement manager. Sales manager who controls the sales force who sell advertising media. Not to be confused with ADVERTISING MANAGER.

Advertisements (Hire Purchase) Act 1967. Regulates advertisements giving hire-purchase terms, as in contractual wording of coupons, especially in off-the-page direct response marketing advertisements which must state total cost of instalments.

advertising. The means of making known in order to sell goods and services (AA); presenting the most persuasive possible selling message to the right prospects for the product or service at the lowest possible cost (IPA); the origination and/or communication of ideas about products in order to motivate people towards purchase (Bernstein).

advertising agency. Group of specialists shared by clients (accounts) for the planning, creation and placing of advertisements. Originated as commission earning space brokers for newspapers some 200 years ago. They are still legally considered as agents of the media, not clients. The custom of the trade is that the 'agent acts as principal' meaning the agency, and not the client, is legally responsible for paying bills. As newspaper printing permitted different sizes of type and reproduction of pictures, space brokers competed by offering creative services. The modern service agency then emerged and developed further after Second World War with provision of marketing and market research services, followed by the advent of commercial TV. Today, full service agencies have to compete with variety of A LA CARTE, creative and many specialist agencies plus MEDIA INDEPENDENTS. About 600 agencies in UK of which under half, but representing bulk of the billings, belong to IPA. A recent development has been to move into PR. Specialist agencies deal with recruitment, sales promotion, direct response marketing, sponsorship, business-to-business, financial, etc.

Advertising Agency Register. Provides prospective clients with video presentations of advertising agencies, plus literature and sales aids. Saves client extensive shopping around.

Advertising Association, The. 1926. Federation of advertising bodies and spokesman for the combined advertising industry. Originated from National Vigilance Committee. It pioneered voluntary controls in 1930s under Russell Chapman. The AA published the British Code of Standards in Relation to the Advertising of Medicines and Treatments (1948); ran the Advertisement Investigation Committee until the independent Advertising Standards Authority was set up in 1962; launched professional exams in the 1930s, now absorbed in CAM of which it is a constituent member; it also has a large library; conducts research into advertising expenditure and has contributed to the dialogue with the European Commission over advertising standards and controls.

advertising awareness research. As conducted on the London Underground with pre-research and post-research into brand awareness as a result of advertising. In one survey conducted by Survey and Fieldwork, 600 Underground travellers were interviewed regarding the Tube Car Panel campaign run for two months. Spontaneous brand awareness rose from 1% to 14%, prompted brand awareness from 2% to 30%.

Advertising Creative Circle. Members are mostly agency creative personnel. It makes an annual award.

Advertising Film and Videotape Producers' Association. Trade association of commercial film and video producers and directors.

advertising funded. A publication which partly or totally depends on advertisement revenue. However, much income is today derived from the cover price if there is one, and few publications depend solely on advertising for their income. Unlike pre-war 'penny' newspapers which were subsidised by advertisers, post-war newsprint, labour and distribution costs required extra income via cover or selling price. It is noticeable that many CONTROLLED CIRCULATION journals have developed a cover price or subscription sales, e.g. *Marketing, Marketing Week, PR Week*.

advertising manager. In-house buyer and controller of advertising and person who liaises with the account executive of an advertising agency. Now largely absorbed in the duties of BRAND or PRODUCT MANAGER. *See also* ADVERTISEMENT MANAGER.

advertising property. Unique value built into a product so that it can be exploited. Integral part of the product including perhaps its exclusive container. Shredded Wheat biscuits, Polaroid camera, Bang and Olufsen equipment are good examples.

advertising speciality. Give-aways, e.g. diary, key ring, identified by advertiser's name, logo, trademark.

Advertising Standards Authority. 1962. Succeeded the Advertising Investigation Department of the Advertising Association which originated from National Vigilance Committee of 1926. It is financed by levies on advertising collected by the ADVERTISING STANDARDS BOARD OF FINANCE and has an independent chairman and committee of members serving in their individual capacity. The ASA administers the BRITISH CODE OF ADVERTISING PRACTICE and BRITISH CODE OF SALES PROMOTION PRACTICE, both influenced by the INTERNATIONAL CODE OF ADVERTISING

PRACTICE. It invites public with well-known 'tick' advertisements to submit written complaints and monitors current advertising. It has a number of specialist advisory committees, publishes a free monthly, *ASA Case Report*, describing complaints investigated and decisions taken and supplies educational videos on self-regulatory system. *See* COMMITTEE OF ADVERTISING PRACTICE (CAP). Eighth edition of BCAP published December 1988. Brook House, Torrington Place, London, WC1E 7HN.

Advertising Standards Board of Finance. 1974. Collects surcharge of 0.1% of gross media rates charged on press, outdoor, cinema and direct mail advertising from advertising agents and media owners to finance ADVERTISING STANDARDS AUTHORITY.

Advertising Statistics Yearbook. Contains statistics of advertising expenditure including breakdowns of expenditure by medium and by type. Annual, The Advertising Association, London.

advertorials. Form of issue advertising, as used by Mobil Oil in USA, when space is taken on leader page to position an organisation regarding an economic, social or political issue. Can also be used to promote a case against media bias or misreporting.

advocacy/issue advertising. Corporate advertising to present a case or position a company in respect of issues of the day such as pollution, environmental problems or hostile legislation.

AEO. *See* ASSOCIATION OF EXHIBITION ORGANISERS.

aerial advertising. Different types of advertising in the sky depending on legislation which may ban low flying aircraft or the use of a single engine aircraft over towns. Forms include: skywriting with smoke; trailed banners; illuminated messages on wings of night-flying aircraft; advertisements projected onto clouds and two or three aircrafts linked together with banners. Goodyear airships with illuminated public announcements;

tethered balloons; HOT AIR BALLOONS are the most recent examples. Fuji films have used an airship painted in their green and red house colours, making it very conspicuous. Airship Industries hire airships to advertisers.

after market. After a product or service has been sold, all those means of satisfying the customer, maintaining goodwill, encouraging recommendations, and achieving repeat or renewal sales, including sales of accessories. Includes guarantees, promises of good performance, service manuals, servicing, spare parts, and special PR efforts such as customer magazines and clubs. Having back-up services may be an important part of advertising.

AFVPA. *See* ADVERTISING FILM AND VIDEOTAPE PRODUCERS' ASSOCIATION.

AGB. Audits of Great Britain.

AGB Buyer Ratings. Research system which can reduce advertising expenditure. It improves TARGETING of TV commercials by helping buyers to choose AIRTIME according to the audience's purchases instead of their SOCIAL GRADES. The performance of a commercial can be checked against desired audience. It guides a buyer's prediction of programmes and day-parts that are most likely to have the highest proportion of purchasers of particular products. Data is continuous.

AGB Market Track Attwood Service. Conducted by AGB Market Information, a continuous CONSUMER PANEL of 4,300 homes measures purchases of fruit, vegetables, dairy products, fish and shellfish, cakes and pastries, morning foods, eating out, cut flowers and pot plants, cigarettes, DIY products, gardening products, light bulbs and fittings. Panel members complete pre-coded diaries and sent these back to AGB each week. The diaries record product bought, price paid and shop used. Monitors trends in market structure by brand, retailer, trade sector, price band, product sector, pack size, etc. Reports two weeks after period end.

AGB Market Track Home Audit Service. Conducted by AGB Market Information, a rotating sample of 35,000 homes reports for 6 quarters on ownership and acquisition of products, with special representation of newly-weds, recent movers, and new homes. Homes are recruited for personal visit, and subsequent audits use post, telephone and personal visits. It is weighted to be representative of the total UNIVERSE of homes. The markets measured are major kitchen appliances, small electrical appliances, home entertainment, heating and insulation, fittings and furniture, DIY and gardening equipment, telephones, travel and tourism, slimming classes, pet ownership. Trends in market structure are monitored by brand retailer, trade sector, fuel type, price band and product sector. Data are produced quarterly. Reports for the latest 8 quarters are sent 8 weeks after period end. Ownership Reports are produced annually.

AGB Market Track Lek-Trak Service. Conducted by AGB Market Information, a retail audit collected from all sectors of the electrical trade and aggregated to estimate total market. Every two years there is a census of independents, from which representative sample recruited. Data collected every four weeks. AGB HOME AUDIT data used to gross up to provide an estimate of the total market. Lek-Trak database holds data on over 30,000 models. Markets measured are large kitchen appliances, small kitchen appliances, home entertainment, personal appliances. Reports are sent every 4 weeks after period end.

AGB Market Track PPI Service. Conducted by AGB Market Information, a continuous panel of 11,600 individuals aged 5–79. Information on some products only collected from adult members. Children complete pre-coded diary which lists all the major brands. They record only the number of packs bought: assumed they buy smallest common pack size at recommended price. Adults record product bought, price paid and shop used. Survey measures purchases of confectionery, snacks, crisps and nuts, soft drinks, take-away alcohol, batteries and torches, greetings cards and calendars, dry cleaning, paperback books. Results are grossed to represent total population. Bi-monthly reports.

AGB Market Track Recall Service. Conducted by AGB Market Information, a continuous survey of 200 individuals aged 16 + interviewed every two weeks, totalling 52,000 individuals each year. Measures purchases of haircare, colour cosmetics, women's and men's toiletries, sun care products, OTC medicines and flowers. Individuals are interviewed about purchases in the previous two weeks. 72% of the sample are women since they account for the majority of purchasing in the markets measured. The results are weighted to represent the adult population. Bi-monthly reports.

AGB Market Track TPCI Service. Conducted by AGB Market Information, a continuous weekly panel of 10,000 individuals aged 13 + measures purchases of haircare, bathroom toiletries, sanitary protection, artificial sweeteners, visits to and by hairdressers. Panelists complete weekly diaries recording products bought, price paid and shop used. These diaries are returned weekly. The panel consists for 60% of women who account for most of the purchasing in the markets measured. The results are grossed-up to represent total population. Reports 2 ½ weeks after period end.

agency catalogue. MAIL ORDER catalogue, e.g. Littlewoods, supplied to agents who earn commission by selling catalogue items on cash or credit terms, or operate mail order clubs.

aggregating. Adding together pre-coded or coded answers to a marketing research questionnaire to produce quantitative results.

AH. Accent height of a typeface, which may vary from one typefounder to another according to the amount of white space above and below character. *See also* KPH and PH.

AIDA. Well-known formula standing for attention, interest, desire, action to which a fifth element, conviction, is sometimes inserted after 'desire'. These elements may be achieved by a combination of contributory factors such as headline, selling points, text copy, illustration(s), layout, typography, size, shape or position of space and colour or choice of medium.

aided recall. In research, a means of obtaining answers from respondents such as cards bearing MASTHEADS of publications during a READERSHIP SURVEY. *See also* RECOGNITION SURVEY.

air. 1. Broadcast a TV commercial. 2. White space or daylight in layout of advertisement or printwork.

air date. Date when TV or radio commercial is to be broadcast.

Air Miles. A novel TRADING STAMP scheme, launched November 1988, and largely linked with British Airways, where vouchers are being redeemed for air travel. The scheme started with some 15 companies giving vouchers on purchases including Burton Group, Shell UK, Sketchley, British Gas and others.

airbrush, airbrushing. Mechanical tool which sprays ink or paint to retouch photographs or to produce shaded effect.

AIRC. *See* ASSOCIATION OF INDEPENDENT RADIO CONTRACTORS.

airport corridors. Approach roads to airports which offer prime sites for posters such as 64 sheets and BULLETIN BOARDS.

airtime. Advertisement time on commercial radio or TV.

airtime buyer. Agency executive who books time for a commercial on radio or TV.

aisle arch. Advertising display above the aisle in supermarkets.

alcoholic drinks. The British Code of Advertising Practice has a whole Section on advertisements for alcoholic drinks which should be studied carefully by anyone concerned with the advertising of such products. In particular, the Code sets out 16 rules which should be observed. Examples: No advertisement should suggest that the femininity or attractiveness of women is enhanced by drinking or by the choice of a particular drink; advertisements for drink should not suggest the enhancement of mental ability or physical capacity. In any advertisement which features sportsmen, particular care is required to avoid the implication being drawn that their performance, or success, is related to their alcohol consumption.

align. Correction on proof to straighten irregular lines of type or characters.

alignment. Arrangement of type and/or illustrations in a layout to justify horizontally or vertically. *See* JUSTIFICATION.

allocation. Division of advertising APPROPRIATION for different ABOVE-THE-LINE and BELOW-THE-LINE purposes plus production costs.

AMSO. *See* ASSOCIATION OF MARKET SURVEY ORGANISATIONS.

ANA. *See* ARTICLE NUMBER ASSOCIATION.

analine ink. Volatile, quick-drying printing ink, as used in FLEXOGRAPHY.

analine printing. *See* FLEXOGRAPHY.

animated bulletin boards. Specially constructed solus outdoor advertising site which has stand-out three-dimensional effects, such as a replica of a product.

animatics. 1. Video method of pre-testing advertisements using a moving cartoon of visual ideas. Slides may also be used. 2. Moving animated or cartoon effects in TV commercial.

animation. Cartoon effects as used in films, videos, TV commercials, action being produced by sequence of numerous drawings filmed and then projected as a moving picture. Not limited to animals of the Mickey Mouse type. *See also* COMPUTER GRAPHICS.

answerprint. Master print or final stage of a TV film.

appeal. Buying motive to which advertisement is aimed.

approach. Treatment of advertisement copy, e.g. factual, hardsell, softsell, emotional, bargain, humorous.

appropriation. The advertising budget. *See* the following methods of deciding total expenditure: ARBITRARY, BUILD-UP, COMPETITOR'S ADVERTISING, COMPOSITE, ELASTICITY, HISTORICAL, NEW PRODUCT, PERCENTAGE OF ANTICIPATED TURNOVER, QUANTIFICATION, RESIDUAL, TARGET SUM.

aquatint. Intaglio printing process that gives reproduction of even or graded tones.

aquatones. *See* COLLOTYPE. Process using fine-screen gelatin-coated plate for OFFSET-LITHO printing.

arbitrary method. Way of deciding advertising appropriation without making serious calculation. What the advertiser thinks he can afford.

area sampling. Form of RANDOM, interval or probability sampling in which the country is divided into areas or CLUSTERS. Reduces costs as respondents can be found more quickly. Also, it is useful in countries where statistical details such as Census figures and Electoral Rolls are lacking, and research can be concentrated on urban areas.

arena advertising. Display panels around perimeter of sports arena, visible to both spectators and TV viewers.

armchair shopping. Synonym for MAIL-ORDER trading or DIRECT RESPONSE marketing. Catalogues and off-the-page ads bring the shop into the home.

art paper. High grade, coated and polished paper. Sometimes called enamelled or cast-coated. The best quality is made from esparto grass with china clay coating. Can be one-sided for decorating packages such as chocolate boxes.

Article Number Association. Body which promotes the use of BAR CODING, and has a code of practice for use of bar codes by manufacturers and distributors.

artistic work. According to the COPYRIGHT, DESIGNS AND PATENTS ACT 1988, an artistic work means (a) a graphic work, photograph, sculpture or COLLAGE, irrespective of artistic quality, (b) a work of architecture being a building or a model for a building, (c) a work of artistic craftsmanship.

artistic works, advertising of. Under Section 63 of the Copyright, Designs and Patents Act 1988, it is not an infringement of copyright in an artistic work to copy it, or to issue copies to the public, for the purpose of advertising the sale of the work.

ASA. *See* ADVERTISING STANDARDS AUTHORITY.

ASBOF. *See* ADVERTISING STANDARDS BOARD OF FINANCE.

ascender. Vertical stroke of letters above x-height as in b, d, f or k.

ashcanning. Inferring in an advertisement that a rival product is inferior and only worth discarding. Knocking copy. Denigration is an offence against the British Code of Advertising Practice.

ASS. *See* ASSOCIATION OF SOCCER SPONSORS.

assembled negative. Combination of line and halftone copy for making litho plate.

Association for Business Sponsorship of the Arts. Advises members who seek sponsors and encourages commercial sponsorship of the arts. Encourages media to give credit to sponsorships. Has achieved considerable increase in arts sponsorship.

Association of British Directory Publishers. Trade association for directory publishers. Maintains standards in an area where there have been dubious practices by unscrupulous publishers, some of whom extracted payments for prompt payment for entries in non-existent directories.

Association of Business Advertising Agencies. Trade association representing business-to-business advertising agencies. Aims to protect such agencies from competition by general consumer agencies, to increase awareness of specialist business agencies, and to raise their creative standards.

Association of Distributors of Advertising Material. 1988. Represents free newspapers approved by VERIFIED FREE DISTRIBUTION and door-to-door leaflet distributors. In the mid-80s leaflets distributed with free newspapers quadrupled to 4m a year.

Association of Exhibition Organisers. Trade association which aims to maintain standards of exhibition management. Promotes development of exhibitions as a major advertising medium.

Association of Free Newspapers. Upholds and promotes standards of free newspapers and their proprietors, and effectiveness of free newspapers as an advertising medium.

Association of Independent Radio Contractors. Trade association of commercial radio companies appointed by the Independent Broadcasting Authority (or any other body resulting from new legislation). Copy control is currently handled by a joint AIRC/ITCA secretariat.

Association of Mail Order Publishers. 1970. Trade association representing those who conduct direct response marketing of books, magazines, gramophone records, cassettes and CDs by post. It has own mail order publishers' authority which administers code of practice.

Association of Market Survey Organisations. Trade association representing market research survey companies. It has a Code of Standards.

Association of Media Independents. 1981. Represents media independents. Members must be recognised for commission purposes by ITCA, NPA and PPA and must accept BCAP, and be of sound financial standing. Remuneration of media independents is usually in the form of a consultancy fee, but some may retain the commission system.

Association of Outdoor Advertising Specialists. Trade association of outdoor advertising consultants and suppliers. Constituent body of JICPAR.

Association of Point of Sale Advertising. Represents interests of producers of POS material.

Association of Soccer Sponsors. 1988. Formed by companies which sponsor football, especially individual teams. Seeks to foster interest in football such as through increased attendances at matches.

Association of Viewdata Information Providers. Trade association of organisations which supply pages of information for PRESTEL.

association test. Measures correct identification of brand names, slogans, advertising themes.

Astra. Satellite used by Sky Television and W. H. Smith television. It operates from Luxembourg and is outside any licensing process approved by the British Government. Astra has 16 channels and was launched from French Guiana in December 1988.

Atex. Kodak direct input computerised typesetting system widely used in modern newspaper offices, replacing foundry for letter-press printed newspapers. Combines text, graphics, display ads, classifieds in single full-page electronic production.

attention factors. Allowances made to BARB TV audience figures to cover distraction or breaks in viewing.

attention value. In recall tests and TRACKING STUDIES a measure of respondent's memory of advertisements.

attitude battery. Study in which respondents are given statements and asked with which they agree or disagree. An analysis shows attitude patterns and motives.

attitude research. Measures attitudes towards or opinions of an organisation. Continuous surveys reveal shifts of attitude over time.

audience delivery plan. Method of selling cinema advertising by delivery of an agreed audience total in a specific ISBA region(s) for an agreed cost. To qualify, advertiser must use all screens within an ISBA ITV Region. The premium rate applies to all London/TVS campaigns. Marplan provides continuous monthly audit of all UK audiences. From these figures specific campaign achievements can be calculated for each month of the advertising schedule, with the statement of audience figures being supplied in arrears.

audience loyalty. As achieved by a popular radio or TV programme. Can be valuable to an advertiser who wishes to reach a large regular audience.

audience measurement. Results of research which quantifies and qualifies those who watch TV programmes (BARB) and radio programmes (JICRAR).

audience share. Proportion of viewer's total viewing time devoted over a period to a particular channel. As the number of channels increases via satellite and cable, the audience share lessens as viewing becomes more fragmented. One aspect of the DE-MASSIFICATION of the media.

audit bin. *See* DUSTBIN CHECK.

Audit Bureau of Circulations. 1931. As from January 1989 the ABC issues monthly audited circulation figures. Previously it had concentrated on six monthly averages with a month-by-month breakdown. This was provoked by individual newspapers announcing estimates of previous week's or month's average sales. Certifies audited net sales of member publications based on audited circulation figures submitted by publishers. Not to be confused with readership figures, which include readers other than buyers and are therefore higher, as estimated following a research commissioned by JICNARS, who publish readership figures.

audited net sale. Average net sale of a newspaper/magazine excluding free copies. *See* AUDIT BUREAU OF CIRCULATIONS.

auto kerning. In phototypesetting, automatic closing of space where ASCENDERS overlap X-HEIGHT of next character.

automated inserting. Mechanical method of placing inserts into newspapers and magazines as introduced by the Mirror Group and the *Financial Times*.

autopage. In litho printing, computer positioning of headlines, sub-heads, text and rules.

average frequency. In commercial TV, average number of exposures/impacts per unit of a defined audience group covered. Similar to OPPORTUNITY TO SEE (OTS).

average hours. Average length of time spent listening to radio or a particular station.

$$\frac{\text{Total Hours}}{\text{Reach}} = \text{Average Hours}$$

AVIP. *See* ASSOCIATION OF VIEWDATA INFORMATION PROVIDERS.

azerty. Keyboard arrangement with accents used in French speaking countries, unlike the standard QWERTY keyboard.

B

B series/sizes. ISO range of paper sizes for large print jobs such as posters.

baby boomers. Those who have grown up since the baby boom of the 60s. *See also* BABY BUSTERS.

baby busters. Generation which has followed baby boomers of the 60s. Fewer births resulted in school closures and towards the turn of the century the sale of houses, furnishings, etc. will be threatened as fewer homes are required.

back-checking. Means of checking the delivery of MAILDROPS by door-to-door distributors, e.g. D.A.S.H. (Distribution Assured Services to Households) operated by Direct Delivery Systems Ltd, Hove. A postcard is sent to those selected through random selection by computer of all postcodes in a defined distribution area, asking if promotional material is received. As an incentive to return the card, it is entered for a monthly prize. Distribution of free newspapers is monitored by inspectors who make spot checks.

back end. Procedures necessary to complete direct response transaction. Also, with record and book clubs or mail order clubs, record of buyer's subsequent purchases after enrolment.

back selling. Promotion of goods of secondary suppliers to those who incorporate them in finished goods. Their identity is often unknown to the final buyer. Advertising may be aimed at the final buyer to encourage specification of a component or ingredient.

back-to-back coupons. Disaster situation when couponed ads are printed on succeeding pages so that they cancel each other out. Can involve more than 7% of ads. The publisher is unaware of eventual copy when space orders are accepted and pages made up.

balloons. *See* HOT-AIR BALLOONS, INFLATABLES.

banded pack. Two or three product units, e.g. bars of chocolate or soap, individual packs of cereals, or cartons of toothpaste, banded together and sold at special price or one unit free.

bangtail envelopes. Envelopes with extra large perforated deep flap or stub which may serve as an order form, to give extra information, provide a competition entry form, or means of giving addresses of friends. Used in DIRECT MAIL.

banknotes, reproduction of. Apart from illegality there is the problem of reproductions being passed off as real currency. This problem occurred once among foreign seamen in the London docks when a banknote was reproduced on an orange wrapper.

bar coding. Method of printing vertical EAN BAR CODES on packs which are read by a cashier at the check-out using an electronic pen or fixed device. Magazines are also bar coded. *TV Times* has 13 regional editions individually coded. The bar coding informs the till of item and price and records stock movement and stock levels. *See also* PINSTRIPE.

BARB. *See* BROADCASTERS' AUDIENCE RESEARCH BOARD.

BARB Establishment Surveys. Annual surveys conducted by BROADCASTERS' AUDIENCE RESEARCH BOARD to establish data on TV advertisement costs, population profiles of ITV areas, TV ownership, reception capabilities, etc.

base artwork. Artwork that needs extra elements such as half-tone positives before a litho plate can be made.

base film. Basic material for contact film in litho plate-making to which film positives are stripped.

baseline. 1. Imaginary line on which bases of capital letters rest. 2. SIGNATURE SLOGAN or STRAPLINE at the foot of an advertisement. It may be a standard slogan for all campaigns, or different ones for different campaigns.

batchfile technique. Variations on original shape of a bodytext face, e.g. bold, shadow, outline, contour, achieved by running options through a digital typesetter.

BCAP. *See* BRITISH CODE OF ADVERTISING PRACTICE.

BDMA. *See* BRITISH DIRECT MARKETING ASSOCIATION.

BDMA/Post Office Direct Marketing Awards. Annual awards in different categories for direct marketing campaigns.

BDMU. BRITISH DIRECT MAIL USERS' ASSOCIATION.

BEAB mark. Incorporates BSI KITEMARK and shows that a product has been tested by British Electrotechnical Approvals Board and conforms to BS standard given in the mark. Applies to domestic electrical equipment and electronic equipment.

beanstalk. POINT-OF-SALE display consisting of stack of trays or shelves.

BECA. *See* BRITISH EXHIBITION CONTRACTORS ASSOCIATION.

behaviour selling. A way of selling which produces particular behaviour. Effects of culturally coercive pressures, e.g. applauding performance, keeping quiet in a library, acting reverently in a holy place, obeying orders from a senior or superior.

behavioural sciences. Sciences concerning psychology, sociology and anthropology. These are closely related to marketing research.

behavioural segmentation. Division of consumers on basis of buying motives. *See* SEGMENTATION.

Behaviourbank. Offered by direct mail agency Mardev, and based on twice yearly national shoppers survey. It consists of value added lifestyle databases covering numerous shopper interests and activities and is divided into more than 300 psychographic/family lifestyles (e.g. credit card owners, food and wine interests, goods owned) and demographics (e.g. marital status, age, income, occupations).

below-the-line advertising. Media other than ABOVE-THE-LINE. Includes exhibitions, direct mail, point-of-sale displays, sales literature, give-aways, sponsorships but not public relations.

Benn's Direct Marketing Services Directory. Lists 1,300 service companies and 5,000 business and consumer mailing lists. Access to BDMS Listline. Twice yearly. Tonbridge, Kent.

Benn's Media Directory. Two-volume UK and Overseas world media guide. Lists some 12,000 UK publications. Covers newspapers, magazines, directories, free newspapers, house journals, broadcasting services, media agencies and services, etc. ABC figures, circulation areas, profiles given of UK journals. Tonbridge, Kent, 1846.

Betamax. Sony domestic video system. Not as popular as VHS.

bias. One-sided point of view. Inaccuracy in response to a survey due to a sample not corresponding with the universe. A bias can also be introduced by an interviewer who allows his own views to influence answers.

billboard. Commonly misunderstood term because of the differences in British and American usage. In Britain a billboard is a small board that carries a double crown or quad crown poster as often seen outside a shop. In North America it is a general term for hoardings and outdoor advertising.

bingo card. Reader-service tear out reply card found in CONTROLLED CIRCULATION trade journals.

black plate change. Printing texts of direct response catalogues with different language versions, as necessary with Euro-marketing. The type area must be adequate to accept those translations which occupy more space than the original English.

blanket. In OFFSET-LITHO printing, a rubber blanket covering the blanket cylinder which receives the inked image from plate-cylinder and offsets it on to paper introduced by impression cylinder.

blanket-to-blanket press. Offset-litho printing press in which paper is printed on both sides at the same time by feeding it between two blanket cylinders.

blanking area. White border or edge of poster for standard-size sites.

bleach-out. Photograph from which grey middle tones have been removed to create dramatic black and white effect. A drop-out.

bleed. Printing illustrations or type area to extreme edge of page (or poster) by trimming to give bled-off effect. Artwork and print has to be larger than space or sheet size to permit trimming.

blind product test. PRODUCT PRE-TEST in which respondents compare two or more similar but unidentified products.

blip culture. Information age culture consisting of conflict between conventional concepts and baffling flood of new ideas.

blister pack. BUBBLE CARD as used for packaging small items like medicinal tablets which can be pressed free as required.

block in. Draw in chief areas and reference points when preparing drawings or design.

block-headed polythene envelopes. *See* POLYTHENE ENVELOPES.

blocking-out. In retouching, painting out or airbrushing unwanted parts of a photograph such as an untidy or obtrusive background.

blow-up (n). Very large photographic enlargement as used in showrooms and on exhibition stands.

blow up (v). To enlarge artwork or a photograph.

blue collar workers. The SOCIAL GRADE C^2 representing skilled working class.

blue key. Way of enhancing halftone effects in monopress advertisements. Produces pure black and white plus mid-tones, using separate overlays for black and white areas.

blues, blueprints. Poor quality proofs for early checking, white lines being printed on blue ground. Ozalids.

board. Pasteboard, cardboard, strawboard, heavyweight paper or card, either one-sheet or made up of layers of paper.

body matter. Text or reading matter as distinct from display lines. *See* TEXT.

bolt-on promotion. SALES PROMOTION scheme that is ready made (e.g. SCRATCH CARD, bingo game), can be bought from a supplier and associated with a product for a special short-term promotion.

bonus pack. Extra large container, e.g. toothpaste tube, cereal packet, aerosol with '10%' or so 'extra' printed on it to promote the product.

book face. Typeface suitable for TEXT matter as distinct from decorative or bold SANS SERIF display faces, e.g. highly readable serif faces such as Times, Plantin and others which are round and have high X-HEIGHT.

book style. Arrangement of paragraphs as found in most books, newspapers and magazines and as opposed to secretarial letter-typing style. The first paragraph of each chapter or article, and first paragraph following a sub-heading, is set FULL-OUT, i.e. not indented. All other paragraphs are indented. Applies to all copy for printing. Achieves legibility and readability. Originated with handwritten Bibles which had decorated DROP CAPITALS for full-out paragraphs. This is still retained when initial drop capitals, or first word or two set in capitals are used in print.

bookmatches, box matches. As given away in clubs, restaurants and hotels, bearing sponsor's name and advertisement. Both advertising and PR medium.

boom issue. Special and often seasonal issue of a magazine used to boost sales and advertising revenue.

booth. Stall or stand at an exhibition.

bounceback. 1. *See* PIGGY-BACKING. 2. Extra premium offer made to customer who has responded to a sales promotion offer.

bounce-back card. Way of calculating response to advertising by asking enquirer questions about his or her job, use of product, other decision makers, etc.

bowl. Enclosed part of letter as in 'b' or 'd'.

BPMA News. Journal of the British Promotional Merchandise Association containing hundreds of promotional and incentive products, and directory of more than 900 BPMA members and product guide. Monthly. Headline Promotions, Maidstone, Kent.

bracketed type. Type in which SERIF is linked to the main stem in an unbroken curve.

BRAD. *See* BRITISH RATE AND DATA.

BRAD Direct Marketing, Lists, Rates and Data. Guide to direct marketing lists and services produced by Maclean Hunter, publishers, and Mardev, direct mail consultants. Monthly. 1988.

brand. Originates from cattle branding. Distinctive name for a product or service. If something has a brand name, it is possible to advertise it using this name. It is difficult to advertise a nameless GENERIC. Brand names are a problem in overseas markets where there can be different and sometimes unfortunate meanings such as Mist meaning 'dung' in German. Euro-branding coupled with cross-frontier satellite TV means that brands have to be acceptable throughout the EC. *See* NATIONAL BRAND.

Brand Activity Reports. Data on advertising activity, giving a record of each press, TV or radio advertisement, available any time from MEAL. Advertisements may be sorted/listed to show: name of advertiser and agency; date of appearance; TV station and channel, radio contractors or publication; spot length or size; time on, special position, use of colour, page number; rate card cost; copy line. Reports are produced as required or as complete analyses on microfiche.

brand awareness. Percentage of consumers who express awareness of brand as revealed by opinion poll.

brand character profile. Human characteristics attributed to products by customers, induced either by personal experience or by advertising. Is it a feminine or masculine product, one for young or old, rich or poor, outdoor life or town dwelling? Is it associated with a particular class, or with those with special interests?

brand expenditure. Amount spent on advertising brands. *See* MEDIA EXPENDITURE ANALYSES LTD (MEAL), KEY REGION RADIO. MEAL publishes reports on advertising expenditure by medium, medium groups, television regions, radio, and area for television and press. Also available on Donovan Data Systems on-line service.

brand image. Character or style which identifies a product and distinguishes it from others. This may be based on a UNIQUE SELLING PROPOSITION, on price or market segments with certain makes of motor-car, particular hotels, brands of perfume, or makes of watch.

brand indicator. As revealed by research into market share and consumer attitudes.

brand leader. Leading brand or market leader in a product group, e.g. best selling tea, coffee, detergent, soap, toothpaste or pet food. Usually revealed by DEALER AUDIT SURVEY.

brand loyalty. Regular and continuous purchase by consumers who reject substitutes or competitive brands. Represents the essential hard core of customers who must be retained. Sales promotion schemes by rivals can undermine brand loyalty. Depends on habit buying. Advertising has to maintain sales as well as increase them. Loyal customers often encouraged when they see ads for their favourite brand.

brand loyalty ladder. Sequence of customer acceptance which advertising can influence in achievement of eventual brand loyalty. Stages or 'rungs' include brand awareness, brand preference.

brand or product manager. *See* ADVERTISING MANAGER.

brand preference. Preference for one brand over others which manufacturers try to obtain through advertising and sales promotion.

brand share. Proportion of the market held by a particular brand. May be based on weight or volume, cash value or number of units sold. Usually determined by DEALER AUDIT RESEARCH.

brand share standardisation. Calculation of effect of a new brand on market shares of existing brands in limited area in a test market, and then relating this effect in the broadscale. Provides an estimate of likely share of the market that a new entrant will gain.

brand strategy. Policy decision regarding kinds of branding to suit different purposes and situations. Should it be a family or umbrella brand name like Cadbury's or Kellogg's? A private own-label brand like Tesco? Various export brands like BAT cigarettes? Or variety of brands not closely associated with manufacturer like Van den Berghs foods?

brand stripping. Purchase or take-over of a company to acquire its brand rather than develop new one.

brand switcher. Person with no brand loyalty who happily purchases best buy such as special offer. *See* CHERRY-PICKING.

brand user image. Type of people who buy the brand.

brand valuation. Methodology created by the Interbrand Group, London, to determine a balance sheet value for a company's brand. A detailed analysis is made of the client's brands, covering history, positioning, support received, market share, competition, past performance, future plans, line extensions, methods of distribution, risks to the brand and so on. Each brand profile is supported by marketing and research detail, samples of packaging and advertisements. All this is reviewed with clients to establish a clear image of the brand's personality and prospects. Working with the client's accountants, financial data is prepared on each brand.

Each brand is scored for attributes which are weighted. The brand score determines the earnings multiple for each brand. These multiples are based on factors such as yield of long term gilts, bid premiums and the weighted cost of capital.

Thus, a brand-by-brand evaluation is calculated, taking into account each brand's trade mark, registered name and other protection, plus any relevant licences or agreements. A valuation assignment takes from two to six weeks.

brand value. Quantification of the value of a brand so that it becomes a long-term value-added asset which can be included in the balance sheet. Ranks Hovis McDougall has added £678m to its business value by evaluating its variety of brand names. Sixty brands were evaluated by Interbrand. The exercise served to defeat take-over bids by enhancing company's net worth, and also its borrowing powers. *See* BRAND VALUATION for methodology.

breakfast TV. Breakfast time TV on BBC, Channel 4 and TV-am.

Bristol board. Smooth finished paper board used for commercial art.

British Code of Advertising Practice. First published 1961 with subsequent revised editions. (8th edn. 1988.) Self-regulatory code which applies to advertisements in newspapers, magazines and other printed publications; indoor and outdoor posters and other outdoor advertisements, including aerial advertisements; cinema and video-cassette commercials; advertisements on viewdata services; and to advertising material such as brochures and leaflets, whether these are mailed, delivered directly, reach the public as inserts in newspapers or other publications, through distribution in shops or at exhibitions, or in other ways. It does not apply to broadcast commercials. All advertisements should be legal, decent, honest and truthful. Administered by the CAP COMMITTEE under the ADVERTISING STANDARDS AUTHORITY which monitors and invites complaints, which it investigates and adjudicates accordingly. Special sections of the Code deal with health claims; hair and scalp products; vitamins and minerals; slimming; cosmetics; mail order; financial services; employment and business opportunities; limited editions; children; media requirements; and alcoholic drinks. There is a special Appendix on cigarette advertising. Among the general rules are ones on unsolicited home visits, comparative and knocking copy.

British Code of Sales Promotion Practice. Also published by CAP Committee and supervised by ASA. Covers free offers; promotions with prizes; charity-linked promotions; etc.

British Direct Mail Users' Association. Trade association representing some 300 users of direct mail.

British Direct Marketing Association. 1976. Formerly British Direct Mail Advertising Association. Represents mostly suppliers of direct response/mail order traders. It awards a Diploma in Direct Marketing and has a code of practice and Telephone Marketing Guidelines. London.

British Exhibition Contractors Association. Trade association representing those who build and equip exhibition stands.

British Exhibition Venues Association. Represents exhibition venues and offers central client enquiry service regarding suitable venues for an event.

British List Brokers Association. Represents majority of British list brokers who supply mailing lists to direct mail users. Publishes Trading Practice Guide and standard terms and conditions of list rental and trading. It also publishes statement on NET NAMES.

British Promotional Merchandise Association. Represents more than 700 suppliers of merchandise and services to organisers of premium and incentive promotional marketing schemes. Sponsors Primex. Publishes *BPMAA News*.

British Rate and Data. Monthly journal listing rate cards, circulation figures, production details of British press, plus data about other media. Maclean-Hunter. London.

broadcast. According to the COPYRIGHT, DESIGNS AND PATENTS ACT 1988 a broadcast means a transmission by wireless telegraphy of visual images, sounds or other information which (a) is capable of being lawfully received by members of the public, or (b) is transmitted for presentation to members of the public. Copyright does not subsist in a broadcast which infringes, or to the extent that it infringes, the copyright in another broadcast or in a cable programme.

Broadcasters' Audience Research Board. 1981. Replaced JIC-TAR, combining JICTAR (ITVA) and BBC surveys of TV audiences. Some 3,000 households are fitted with a set meter to each receiver. This meter marks a paper tape to record the time and channel that is switched on. Panel home also completes weekly diary. This has been or will be adapted to measure VCR, cable, and satellite programmes. The Board publishes weekly Top 10 audience figures, available by press reports, computer tape and through AGB's private viewdata system. *See* PEOPLE METER.

Broadcasting in the 90s: Competition, Choice and Quality. White paper published 8 November 1988. Chief proposals were: ITV is to be replaced by regional Channel Three with reduced public service obligations, no requirement to produce networked programmes, and contracts (subject to suitability tests) to be auctioned. A fifth channel funded by advertising, sponsorship, subscription, is to start 1993. A further, sixth channel, if feasible. British Satellite Broadcasting's three channels are to be joined by two more in 1990. BBC licence fee is to give way to subscriptions. IBA and Cable Authority are to be replaced by Independent Television Authority and regulated by 'light touch'. Commercial radio is to be governed by Radio Authority. Up to 30 new local TV channels, delivered by cable and/or MICROWAVE system, are to open 1991. Channel 4 airtime is to be sold separately from Channel 3. Separate night-time franchise will exist on Channel 3 and on one BBC channel. The legislation is expected by 1990, with effect in 1991.

broadscale. Full scale such as nationally, as when a product is marketed nationally following TEST MARKETING, or after a zoned launch in a limited area of the market.

broadsheet. A large page newspaper as compared with a TABLOID. In direct mail, a large sheet which folds down to a smaller size like a map.

bromide. Photographic print on bromide paper, or a proof from photocomposition on paper instead of film.

BSI Kitemark. A product displaying this mark has been licensed to do so following inspection by the British Standards Institution of the maker's quality control system together with testing of the product. Originated in 1909 when BSI first registered Kitemark as trademark for tramcar rails. *See also* BEAB MARK.

bubble card. BLISTER PACK as used for packaging small items like tablets.

budget. Planned costs for a project. The budget for an advertising campaign is also called APPROPRIATION.

build-up. Period before an exhibition when exhibits arrive and stands are erected, decorated and laid out.

build-up-method. Assembly of advertising appropriation by making allocations to different media and so building up the total budget.

bulkhead. In buses, advertisement position above windows of interior.

bullet. Large decorative dot used in layouts to draw attention to, say, selling points.

bulletin board. A supersite like those offered by More O'Ferrall in national campaigns. Specially constructed large solus outdoor advertising site, not to be confused with small public notices. Panels are usually painted but can also be posters. They may be set off in gardens and floodlit at night. Panels can be moved from site to site under quarterly rotary system.

Buppies. Black YUPPIES.

burst. Short advertising campaign as distinct from regular DRIP.

bus advertising. *See* ILLUMINATED INTERIOR PANELS; L-SIDE; SEE YOU IN BARKING tracking study; T-SIDE; VINYL.

bus shelter advertising. Various package schemes offered by contractors such as More O'Ferrall, Adshel, Mills & Allen etc.

business card advertisement. Small ad resembling business card.

business press. Journals read by businessmen such as the *Financial Times, Wall Street Journal, Investor's Chronicle* and *The Economist*.

Business Television Network. Live, interactive, private satellite TV broadcasting network, transmitting to any or all Crest Hotels throughout UK. Useful for announcing new products or advertising campaigns to sales force or distributors by means of simultaneous presentation. Business Television Corporation, London.

business-to-business advertising. Advertising which sells business services and equipment to businesses. Has specialist agencies with own trade association ASSOCIATION OF BUSINESS ADVERTISING AGENCIES. Media may include trade and business press, trade exhibitions and direct response mailings.

buzz words. Expressions which represent current trends and situations, but may be short-lived. Also, in advertising, clichés which may seem banal but which work in copy, e.g. now, at last, unique, free.

C

C type. Kodak photographic colour print made directly from negative.

Cable Authority, The. 1984. Licenses cable TV operators and overseas programme services provided.

cable net. Cable TV services in various countries which receive satellite TV programmes.

cable programme. According to the COPYRIGHT, DESIGNS AND PATENTS ACT 1988, a cable programme means any item included in a cable programme service which means a service and consists wholly or mainly in sending visual images, sounds or other information by means of a telecommunications system, otherwise than by wireless telegraphy, for reception (a) at two or more places (whether for simultaneous reception or at different times in response to requests by different users), or (b) for presentation to members of the public, and for which is not, or so far as it is not, accepted by or under provisions (further specified).

cable television. TV programmes delivered to homes by fibre-optic cable that is lain in the road. Offers a variety of programmes including the ones received by satellite. Popular in the USA because the system offered better programmes. Slow to develop in UK because of superiority of existing BBC/TV programmes. Cable TV is now received in 14% of households. In 1988, Benelux and Scandinavian countries were more heavily cabled than Spain, Italy, France and UK. Satellite TV via cable increased to home market in 1989. *See* MICROWAVE TELEVISION and *broadcasting in the 90s*.

CACI Market Analysis. *See* ACORN. Also publishes mid-census population figures.

calendar. Advertising/PR medium which keeps the company name in a prominent place. Some companies print their own (e.g. Pirelli), others have name overprinted on beautiful stock calendars supplied by firms such as Bemrose and Eversheds.

calendered. A paper given a finished or polished surface by passing it through rollers or calenders. Super-calendered is used for magazines.

call offs. In an advertisement, copy which describes parts of an illustration. It is usually set around illustration and connected by lines to the parts described.

call report. *See* CONTACT REPORT.

callback. Repeat call made by a researcher because the respondent was absent, as with random sample when a given number of attempts must be made to interview a named respondent before a substitute may be used. In some research, as when a product is left on trial, there will be a callback.

CAM. *See* COMMUNICATION, ADVERTISING AND MARKETING EDUCATION FOUNDATION.

camera lucida. 'Lucy' means of drawing layouts, permitting picture to be drawn in different sizes.

camera-ready copy. Line artwork and typesetting arranged as complete artwork ready to be photographed for litho plate-making.

Campaign. Weekly advertising journal. Haymarket Press, London, 1968.

CAP Committee. *See* COMMITTEE OF ADVERTISING PRACTICE.

capital letters. 'Caps'. To be used sparingly in editorial material, but can be used for emphasis in advertising. However, wording becomes illegible if, for instance, a whole paragraph is set in 'caps'.

caps. *See* CAPITAL LETTERS.

caption board. Artwork used when making titles for videotapes.

caption or legend. Descriptive wording to explain an illustration.

car card. Advertisement displayed in compartment of under-ground train, usually above the windows. *See* TUBE CAR PANELS.

card rates. Media advertisement rates as stated on the RATE CARD, that is without any special discounts or deals.

cartonboard. Well-finished board for making cartons for products.

cartoons. Drawings of a sequence of actions to produce a movie effect for films or TV commercials. Also, for press advertisements or instructions with products, cartoon strip demonstrating stage by stage how to use a product. *See* ANIMATION.

cartridge. Hard matt-surface paper, originating from gun cartridges, used as drawing paper, or for litho-printing and especially for posters.

cash awards. SALES PROMOTION method as when cash is given to people possessing a product when called on or stopped in the street. Has been used to promote domestic products, newspapers, matches.

cash dividends, refunds. Sales promotion method when cash is paid for collecting tokens or stamps supplied with goods or printed on package.

cash premium coupons, vouchers. Representing a discount when redeemed by making a purchase. Printed in press, or MAIL DROP or on package. MALREDEMPTION occurs when stores accept vouchers for goods other than the ones intended. Manu-facturers attempt to overcome this by insisting on the voucher that it can be redeemed only for the product being promoted, but supermarket chains often ignore this provided they stock the promoted line.

cash refunds. *See* MONEY REFUNDS.

cast-off. In typography, calculating the type-setting required by the copy and to fit the space.

catalogue marketing. In DIRECT RESPONSE marketing, selling from a catalogue. This started in the USA in the mid-19th century by Sears, Roebuck and Montgomery Ward selling almost anything by mail to Mid-Western farmers. It is led in Britain by Moores, Great Universal Stores, Freemans. Big catalogues, known as WISH BOOKS, are now replaced by more specialised ones, while Innovations and similar catalogues have emerged. The Next Directory receives 90% of orders by telephone, and is a hard-back catalogue with swatches of material, and a 48-hour delivery service.

catch phrase. An advertising SLOGAN or JINGLE which becomes so familiar that it becomes part of the language as a popular saying. 'Nice one, Cyril' has been used in TV commercials for a baker and a banker.

catchline. SLOGAN, SIGNATURE SLOGAN, strapline, or tagline.

CAVIAR. *See* CINEMA AND VIDEO INDUSTRY AUDIENCE RESEARCH.

ccm. Column centimetre. Unit for measuring depth of column in press advertising, minimum space usually 3ccm.

CCTV. *See* CLOSED CIRCUIT TELEVISION.

cel. Abbreviation of cellulose acetate. Transparent sheet used for drawing cartoons.

Census of Distribution. Conducted 1951, 1971. Covers the number, size, turnover, location of shops and other retail outlets.

Census of Population. Complete count of British population conducted every ten years by the Office of Population Censuses and Surveys. The first census was in 1801. The data collected cover place of birth, economic activity, housing, change of address over specified period, and higher education qualifications.

Census of Production. Conducted since 1910, with annual sample censuses and a full census every three or four years. It details size and number of firms in an industry.

centralised media buying. Introduced in 1988 by Saatchi and Saatchi to handle media buying (but not media planning). Zenith services agencies in Saatchi and Saatchi group.

centre. Typographical or proof correction instruction to place or move copy to middle of space.

centrefold spread (or centre spread). Middle pages of a publication which open flat as in wire-stitched magazine and can be printed right across. Naturals. Facing pages in middle of a SIGNATURE.

Centry. Census retrieval. PINPOINT database of census information. *See* GEOPIN. Contains entire 1981 census databases— over 5,000 'bits' of information for 130,000 enumeration districts. Clients may select any combination of census variables. Has 104 census variables.

CH. Capital height. Metric type sizes are expressed 18mm CH (= 72pt).

Channel 5. New commercial network to be launched in January 1993. Due to vagaries of transmission capabilities, this channel is not likely to be wholly national and will probably cover the Kent-Sussex coast and parts of the West Country, Essex and certain other areas.

Channel Three. New name for ITV under Broadcasting White Paper, with station contracts auctioned instead of licensed.

character. A single printing letter or symbol.

character count. Total number of type characters and spaces in copy to be printed.

character merchandising. Use of celebrities for promotional purposes.

characters per inch. Measurement unit of type in a line or column width.

characters per pica. Methods of COPYFITTING or CASTING OFF by average number of characters per pica, a pica being 12 points. (POINT SYSTEM consists of 72 points to the inch).

characters per second. Speed of a photo-typesetter.

charity promotions. SALES PROMOTION schemes in which contributions to a charity are given instead of gifts for customers. Tokens with cash value may be printed on packs and these are to be collected so that charity receives the benefit.

Chartered Institute of Marketing. Gained Royal Charter in March 1989. Professional body for those engaged in or studying marketing. Holds Certificate and Diploma examinations. Publishes *Quarterly Review of Marketing*, *Marketing Business*. Has College of Marketing which runs courses throughout year. Cookham, Maidenhead.

cherry-picking. Selection by shopper of brands with special offers.

Cheshire labels. Specially prepared paper used to print names and addresses and that can be mechanically fixed singly to mailing pieces.

chief wage earner. As may be required by research, senior working member of household. This is normally the oldest related male over 21 in full-time employment; otherwise the oldest related female over 21 in full-time employment.

children and advertising. BCAP Section C.X 1.1 says 'direct appeals or exhortations to buy should not be made to children unless the product advertised is one likely to be of interest to them and one which they could reasonably be expected to afford for themselves'. In 1.2 it says 'advertisements should not encourage children to make themselves a nuisance to their parents, or anyone else, with the aim of persuading them to buy an advertised product'. The Section has 16 rules on the subject, half of which concern safety, (e.g. 2.1 'special care should be taken to avoid the likelihood of children copying any practices which are either inherently unsafe, or likely to become unsafe when engaged in by children. The following paragraphs highlight some particular danger areas in advertisements likely to appeal to children').

children and television advertising. IBA Code of Advertising Standards and Practice has an Appendix 1, 'Advertising and Children', which rules that no commercials must be used which might result in harm to children physically, mentally or morally. It also restricts times when certain products may be advertised. The use of children in commercials must be done in such a way that children are not encouraged to copy dangerous acts. Employment of children in making of advertisements is covered by Children and Young Persons Act, 1933 (Scotland 1937); Education Acts 1944–8; Children (Performances) Regulations 1968, and local authority by-laws made in pursuance of this legislation.

chroma. Purity of colour.

chroma copy. Colour print made without negative.

chroma key slides. Slides with picture outlined by black mask which allows viewers to see the picture as a background behind the TV studio announcer or presenter.

chromo paper. Very heavily coated paper, superior to art paper. Dull or glazed for colour litho.

chromolithography. Many coloured lithoprinting as distinct from the four-colour process so that special colours may be printed. Used for poster printing when more than four inks are used.

CI. Copy instruction when placing press advertisement.

Cibachrome print. High quality colour print from transparency.

cigarette advertising. The advertising of cigarettes, of the components of manufactured cigarettes and of hand-rolling tobacco forms Appendix 1 of the 8th edn. of the BRITISH CODE OF ADVERTISING PRACTICE. It concerns the Cigarette Code which has resulted from discussions between the Department of Health and Social Security, (on behalf of the UK Health Depts), the manufacturers and importers of cigarettes (as represented by the Tobacco Advisory Council and the Imported Tobacco

Products Advisory Council), and the ADVERTISING STANDARDS AUTHORITY.

The ASA's involvement is two-fold. It acts as the final arbiter of the meaning of the rules, and it supervises the pre-clearance procedure for advertisements within the scope of the Cigarette Code, which is operated by the COMMITTEE OF ADVERTISING PRACTICE. There are 14 rules, e.g. 2.1: advertisements should not seek to persuade people to start smoking; 2.7: advertisements should not claim directly or indirectly that smoking is a necessity for relaxation or for concentration; 2.12: no advertisement should appear in any publication directed wholly or mainly to young people. There are also nine guidelines for interpreting the rules. For example, 3.8 (1): people engaged in dangerous activities or occupations should not be depicted smoking while so engaged, nor should it be implied that it is normal for them to smoke, or to smoke a particular brand. Exception was taken to a cigarette advertisement in which a uniformed airline pilot was shown smoking a cigarette. The Cigarette Code does not apply to broadcast commercials since cigarette advertising is not permitted.

cinema advertising. A medium which was popular until arrival of television in the 50s. Tends to be young adults medium. However, during the 1980s the average weekly cinema audiences moved from 0.99m in Jan–Sep 1984 to 1.48m in Jan–Sep 1988, and use of cinema advertising increased in response to CAVIAR and INSIGNIA RESEARCH findings. Annual cinema admissions moved from 64m in 1983 to over 75m in 1988. There are 1,233 screens.

Cinema Advertising Association. Trade association of cinema advertising contractors in UK and Ireland. Has conducted research into composition of cinema-going audience.

Cinema and Video Industry Audience Research. Conducted annually since 1981 by Carrick James Market Research on behalf of CINEMA ADVERTISING ASSOCIATION. Report shows the frequency of cinema-going by age, sex and social grade, the frequency of video watchings, and four year trends.

circulation. Net sale of a publication, that is actual number of copies sold. Less than READERSHIP. Audited net sale figures certified by AUDIT BUREAU OF CIRCULATIONS. The cost per thousand net sale is the cost of advertisement space divided by ABC Figure.

claims matrix mapping. System devised by Rockwell International Corporation, USA, to define advertising claims likely to be most effective. Claims are taken from rival advertisements. The lefthand column of matrix lists the claims. In columns for each advertiser, claims are given order of merit ratings. The claims are then weighted and ranked. The claims are pre-tested to discover chief needs of target audience. Then a full survey is conducted. Finally, rank order of claims and target audience needs are compared to discover differences. These differences indicate claims advertiser should use.

classified advertisements. In the press, 'small ads' with copy run on and classified under headings, sometimes with box numbers. Many publications have phone-in service. Journals like *Exchange and Mart* specialise in classifieds. Usually separate advertisement manager. *See also* SEMI-DISPLAY and DISPLAYED ADVERTISEMENT.

clean proof. Proof with few if any errors needing correction.

close up. Proofreading instruction to delete space between characters or words.

closed circuit television. Narrow casting. TV is confined to location where shot, and not broadcast, or played back on video-tape recorder, or delivered by private land-line. Can be used as advertising medium in shops, hotels, in airliners or on board ship, or at showrooms and exhibitions.

closed-ended question. In a research questionnaire, a question which requires a definite answer such as yes, no, don't know, choice from a list, or agreement or disagreement with a statement. Not an open-ended question where the informant may answer freely.

club line. First line of a paragraph at foot of page, rest of paragraph running on to next page. Can look ugly and is best avoided.

cluster analysis. Used in MARKET SEGMENTATION ANALYSIS to identify a group of consumers with common characteristics in order to provide goods or services to these groups. Applied to gap analysis for finding unfulfilled consumer needs.

clutter. Excessive display of advertisements such as shop signs or estate agency boards.

coding and tabulation. In marketing research, translation of survey replies into numerical codes for automatic or computerised data processing.

coding frame. When compiling marketing research questionnaire, a pattern of likely answers which can be pre-coded so that the answers can be aggregated in categories.

coin reactive. DIRECT MAIL or SALES PROMOTION novelty in which numbers, names or answers are invisible, even though there is no scratch-off ink covering them, but a hidden symbol can be revealed by rubbing with a coin. Venturini (Morley-Cox, Bromley).

coin rub. DIRECT MAIL or SALES PROMOTION device to achieve customer participation. A specially formulated ink used in conjunction with normal four colour printing. When coin rubbed over printed area a hidden number, phrase or image is revealed. *See also* LATEX SILVER SCRATCH OFF. HunterPrint, Corby, Venturini (Morley Cox, Bromley).

cold-air inflatables. Ground-standing giant product replicas as used for exhibitions, product launches, sponsorships. Do not float at end of tether like helium balloons and HELI-BLIMPS.

cold colour. Blue or one containing blue.

cold composition. Computerised typesetting, which does not use hot metal.

cold lists. DIRECT MAIL mailing lists which have no affinity with advertiser.

collage. Abstract art form, pictures being scattered over a surface and fixed to it.

collaretic. Card with a hole for attaching to the neck of a bottle as price tag, or to a sales promotion offer.

collating. Collecting pages of print in page order.

collect and select. SALES PROMOTION scheme where coupons are given with purchases and customers can select gifts. Shell offered coupons plus cash selections from catalogue. Air Miles vouchers qualify for flights and holidays.

collectibles. Goods which are collected such as stamps, coins, medals, pictures, plates, often sold by DIRECT RESPONSE marketing. BRITISH CODE OF ADVERTISING PRACTICE, Section CIX, refers to advertising of collectibles, defining as 'a product advertised in terms of its interest as a collector's item, with the emphasis being placed primarily upon factors such as scarcity or aesthetic quality and not, or not solely, upon practical considerations (e.g. utility)'. Code lays down rules about misleading prospective purchasers 'about the scarcity or about the current, or likely future value of the item'; about 'limited editions' and about articles containing precious metal.

collective mark. Trade mark or name used to identify goods marketed collectively, e.g. Cape, Jaffa, Outspan, Sunkist.

collotype. Screenless gelatin printing process used for reproducing illustrations, especially fine art.

colophon. Publishing inscription at front of publication stating details of author, publisher, printer, copyright, ISBN, date and edition.

colour bars. On four-element process proofs coloured strips which show the density of colour across a sheet.

colour correction. Adjustment of colour values to obtain a correct colour printing.

colour harmony. Four principles: (a) *order* —colour harmony depends on colours being chosen according to a logical plan; (b) *familiarity* —colour combinations most familiar to observer will seem to be most harmonious. They are often based on colour combinations in nature; (c) *similarity* —related colours will have an harmonious effect; (d) *contrast* —good colour combinations are very evident when contrasted with poor or odd ones.

colour magazine, supplement. Colour magazine issued free (but sometimes at extra charge) with many Sunday and Saturday newspapers. Previously only with newspapers like *Sunday Times, The Observer*, and *Sunday Telegraph*, but it was taken up by more popular newspapers such as *Mail On Sunday*'s *You* magazine, and other new ones on Saturdays as well as Sundays in 1988. *The Independent* introduced a monochrome Saturday magazine in 1988.

colour positives. Set of halftone screened positive COLOUR SEPARATIONS.

colour separation. Using filters, separation of full colour pictures into four PROCESS COLOURS to give four films for platemaking.

colour separation overlay. TV method which enables pictures to be projected electronically to create superimposed pictures in constant electronic mural. Provides simultaneous moving or pictorial effects for TV presenters.

colour sequence. Printing order of colours: yellow, magenta (red), cyan (blue), black.

colouring competition. SALES PROMOTION scheme where children can colour open-line pictures. Used by circuses in 30s; cards were delivered door-to-door and free tickets offered to children who coloured such cards so that adults would buy tickets. More recently it has been adopted by supermarkets, and London Zoo placed a colouring ad in the press.

colours, legibility of lettering/type. Coloured characters on coloured backgrounds are decreasingly effective in this order: black on yellow, green on white, blue on white, white on blue, black on white, yellow on black, white on red, white on orange, white on black, red on yellow, green on red, red on green, blue on red. (Derek Keeling).

column inch, centimetre. Depth of column space in a newspaper. Unit for calculating and selling space. *See* CCM.

column rule. In printing, light rule for separating columns.

combination rate. Special space rate for inserting advertisement in more than one publication owned by the same publisher.

Commercial Art Directors Association. 1986. Association of advertising set designers and art directors. Members pool their technical know-how by way of fact sheets.

commercial break. *See* NATURAL BREAK, MINUTAGE LEVELS.

commercial clutter. Excessive advertising which looks untidy and offends public. In 1988 many protests were received about the profusion of estate agents boards on one property and local authorities consequently restricted displays to one board per property.

commercial radio/TV. System, as in Britain, of broadcasting commercials in NATURAL BREAKS with independent programming, as distinct from programmes being sponsored by advertisers and including their own spots. Commercials are limited to a specified number of minutes per hour, usually two-minute breaks or six minutes to the hour. Controversy arose in 1988 over the EC directive for fewer commercials, and the possibility of presenting them in periods rather than interspersing throughout programme.

commercial slot. Time between TV programmes, or NATURAL BREAK in programme, when commercials are transmitted.

commission system. Original method of remunerating advertising agencies, dating from 19th century space broking. Anomalous situation resulting in agency being paid by media, not advertiser, and legal custom of the trade that advertising agency acts as principal and is responsible for debts. At one time rate of commission guaranteed by media owners bodies (NPA, NS, PPA), but it was held to be monopolistic by Office of Fair Trading, November, 1978. Agencies continue to be 'recognised' for commission purposes but commission rates are negotiable. However, many variations on system. Some agencies rebate commission and charge fees based on time and expertise, which is more professional.

Committee of Advertising Practice. Prepares, amends, and observes the BRITISH CODE OF ADVERTISING PRACTICE. It is composed of representatives of the Advertising Association, Association of Free Newspapers, Association of Independent Radio Contractors, Association of Mail Order Publishers, Bus Advertising Council, Cinema Advertising Association, Direct Mail Producers Association, Direct Mail Services Standards Board, Incorporated Society of British Advertisers, Independent Television Association, Institute of Practitioners in Advertising, Institute of Sales Promotion, Newspaper Publishers Association, Newspaper Society, Periodical Publishers Association, Proprietary Association of Great Britain, Scottish Daily Newspaper Society, Scottish Newspaper Publishers Association, Videotex Industry Association, British Direct Marketing, British Sign Association, and Outdoor Advertising Association. Supervised by Advertising Standards Authority. The Committee consists of some 30 people nominated by sponsoring bodies. Four standing sub-committees dealing with health claims, financial advertisements, mail order and sales promotion. *See* COPY PANEL.

Communication, Advertising and Marketing Education Foundation. Combines exams that were formerly run by AA, IPA and IPR. Revised syllabuses in 1988; Certificate of Communication Studies: Marketing, Advertising, Public Relations, Media, Sales Promotion & Direct Marketing, Research and Behavioural Studies; Diploma: Management and Strategy (Core Subject), and two subjects for each specialism from Public Relations Management, Public Relations Practice, Consumer Advertising, Business to Business Advertising, or International Advertising, Sales Promotion Management and Structure and Sales Promotion Practice. Certificate and Diploma examinations are normally taken over two years.

Communication, Advertising and Marketing Graduates Association. 1986. Organisation representing holders of CAM Diploma (MCAM) and CAM Fellows.

communications planner. Media planner who evaluates comparative benefits of MEDIA ADVERTISING, SPONSORSHIP, SALES PROMOTION, PR, etc. Introduced by Saatchi and Saatchi.

community radio. 26 areas named by the IBA with 20 stations operative 1989. Include four London district stations and a Greater London FM and an AM ethnic station. Airport information stations at Heathrow and Gatwick.

comparative, comparison advertising. Admissable when similar items are compared, such as motor-cars in the same price band. It must not contain derogatory 'KNOCKING COPY'.

competitions, prize contests. SALES PROMOTION schemes where tokens or wrappers from products as proof of purchase usually give right to enter. It should conform with the Betting, Gaming and Lotteries Act 1963 and contain an element of skill. Tiebreaker often included to avoid the prize being divided among too many winners. Prize should be acceptable: e.g. motorcars and cash prizes better than holidays which may involve family problems or extra costs and no cash alternative. There should be adequate time for judging. Results should be published.

competitor's advertising method. Way of deciding advertising APPROPRIATION according to expenditure by rivals. Can be used for a new product when promotion costs are uncertain, or to match a competitor. Rival expenditures gleaned from estimates published by MEAL.

Compo Mailer. DIRECT MAIL piece consisting of a letter and envelope, both personalised, and up to three inserts (cards, reply envelopes, order forms, advertising leaflets) all manufactured in one step. Morley-Cox Ltd, Bromley, Kent. *See also* RESPONSE PAK.

composite method. A method of calculating the advertising APPROPRIATION by combining various factors and influences. There are many methods of arriving at appropriation, many of which can be combined.

composite pages. In a newspaper or magazine, those pages devoted to ads on particular subjects such as holidays, mail order offers, gardening or houses for sale. Makes small spaces viable because of market place appeal.

composite print. Commercial TV film or video with both sound and picture combined.

composition sizes. Body or TEXT TYPE smaller than 14 point.

compositor. Printing term, originally meaning one who composed type by hand, placing individual metal type characters in a hand-held 'stick'. In computerised printing it refers to one who composes pages (either as paste-up or on screen) prior to photography and plate-making.

computer graphics. Drawing layouts or other designs by computer for taping and transferring to videotape. Also used for slides. Input using keyboard, graphics tablet and VDU, and transmission to the computer. Image stored on disc, operator selecting colours, typefaces, shapes, and symbols using keyboard or touching VDU screen with electronic 'pen'.

Final image transferred into camera which shoots picture off high definition TV screen.

computer maps. *See* PINPOINT IDENTIFIED NEIGHBOURHOODS, MAPPING.

con. CONDENSED type characters.

concept. The whole advertisement, headline, text, illustrations, coupon.

concept testing. Method of testing new products to estimate consumers' attitudes to it before it is fully developed. Simple description, possibly drawn, and a questionnaire with assessment of intention to buy, supplied to sample. Studies may be repeated.

conceptual differences. Reasons why responses to advertising vary. Is a mailshot better received at home or workplace? Will readers or viewers respond differently according to their understanding of the subject, or the influence of the media, or the COPY PLATFORM?

condensed. Narrow version of a typeface, allowing more characters to the line. Useful for small spaces like boxes or coupons.

consumer benefit. Something added to a product or service which makes it more desirable.

consumer diary. Panel research in which respondents complete diary sheets about items bought, programmes watched or listened to, journeys made as appropriate to survey. Usually form of continuous research. Examples: *see* various AGB surveys.

consumer durables. Household goods having a longer life, higher price and less frequent purchase than consumer goods. Include domestic appliances, furniture, home entertainment, power tools, garden equipment.

consumer goods. Usually described as fast-moving consumer goods (fmcgs). Small unit lines such as typical mass market foods, drinks, toiletries, household products found in super-markets. Usually heavily advertised and dependent on repeat sales to maintain volume factory output.

Consumer Location System. Computerised method of analys-ing people's purchasing, reading and viewing habits, relating to residential neighbourhoods. Developed by Royal Mail.

consumer panel. Local, regional or national panel of recruited respondents. Often consumers but sometimes specialists. The research is continuous with either regular visits by interviewers or diaries submitted to organisers every week. *See* AGB MARKET TRACK ATTWOOD SERVICE and TELEVISION CONSUMER AUDIT. Also, panel of omnibus surveys made up of sets of question-naires on behalf of different sponsors, and for product pre-testing.

consumer participation. Consumer activities beyond purchas-ing consumer goods, such as serving on consumer panels and consumer organisations, and answering questionnaires.

consumer profile. Demographic information concerning buyers of a particular brand compared with that of whole consuming public.

Consumer Protection Act 1987. One of the most important pieces of consumer legislation, implementing in the UK the EEC Product Liability Directive. Amends earlier acts and has Parts on Product Liability, Consumer Safety and Misleading Price Indications. *See* PRICES, MISLEADING. All earlier legislation on prices is repealed. Stringent controls on bogus prices. The Act imposes a general duty on producers and suppliers to sell safe products, and this requirement is additional to any existing safety legislation. Producers, importers and own labellers are liable for unlimited damages for defects which cause injury or death. Proof of either negligence or contractual relationship is not required. Retailers must take care not to sell dubious foreign products such as dangerous Christmas tree lights. If necessary, faulty products must be recalled urgently to avoid offending against the Act.

consumer sovereignty. Power of the consumer to influence manufacturers to satisfy their needs and wants, expressing this through consumer organisations and supported by consumer protection legislation (e.g. CONSUMER PROTECTION ACT 1987) and voluntary controls and advisory bodies.

consumerism. Consciousness of price, performance and quality among buying public, and awareness of misleading advertisements. Pioneered in USA by RALPH NADER and his Nader's Raiders. Represented by CONSUMERS' ASSOCIATION in UK and specialised groups such as Friends of the Earth. It also comprises investigative journalism in press and TV programmes which investigate consumer interests.

Consumers' Association. 1956. Independent non-profit-making body founded by shoppers who required unbiased reports on goods and services. Publishes various *Which* reports on goods and services. Frequently provides spokesmen on consumer interest programmes like Esther Rantzen's *That's Life*.

contact report. Call report by account executive following meeting with client. Sets out brief minutes of the meeting and states decisions taken. Has ruled off column on the right-hand side in which are included initials of person responsible for taking next action regarding each decision. Collected in agency facts book file.

continuity incentive gift. SALES PROMOTION scheme which encourages repeat purchasing like dividend, PICTURE CARDS or other collecting schemes.

continuity premium. SALES PROMOTION scheme which builds brand loyalty and habit buying because of its continuous requirement to collect stamps, tokens or coupons in order to obtain gifts.

continuous tone. Pictures in which there are shades from lightest to darkest tones, including a range of mid-tones, which lends itself to litho printing.

contones. Four-colour continuous tone colour separations made by camera fitted with colour filters.

contour setting. Production of text which follows a shape or contour, this being possible with digital typesetting. While this presents a type mass which is visibly attractive, it can seriously detract from the readability of the text. Too clever design may destroy copy.

contrast. In black and white pictures, the difference between black and white which can create dramatic effect. In typography, contrast can be achieved by use of large and small type, or by bold headlines and sub-headings contrasted against lighter text areas.

Control of Misleading Advertisements Regulations 1988. Gives effect to the EC Directive of Misleading Advertising. The Director General of Fair Trading gives powers to institute a High Court action for injunction prohibiting misleading advertising, always provided that the complainant has failed to obtain satisfaction from a voluntary body such as the ADVERTISING STANDARDS AUTHORITY under the BRITISH CODE OF ADVERTISING PRACTICE. However, the Director has said he will not provide a standing court of appeal for decisions of the ASA.

control question. In a research questionnaire, a question which is inserted to check consistency and honesty of respondent's answers. The question is usually one to which a standard answer may be expected.

controlled circulation. Refers to those journals distributed free of charge to selected recipients plus those who have requested copies on publishers invitation. Most cc journals are trade and technical, and they usually have higher penetration of market than purchased journals. Consequently, publishers have adopted controlled circulation distribution in order to be able to offer advertisers large circulation, justifying high advertisement rate. However, recent trend has been to reduce the free list and build up a subscription list. Sometimes a new magazine will start as a cc and gradually revert to one with a cover price, bookstall sales and postal subscriptions.

convenience product. Product which saves buyer's time or makes life easier, e.g. frozen meals, prepared vegetables, babyfoods.

cool media. Media which invite audience to participate. Films and TV. *See* HOT MEDIA, MCLUHAN, MARSHALL.

co-op mailing. *See* PIGGY-BACKING, but more specifically placing two or more offers in the same envelope with shared mailing costs.

co-operative advertising. 1. Joint advertising campaigns by two or more sponsors. 2. Advertising campaigns on behalf of trade or industry, paid for by levy on members. 3. Support schemes for dealers who are either supplied with standard artwork, or paid part of advertising costs. Also called VERTICAL ADVERTISING.

Copland model (1988). Revaluation and modernisation of poster audience model conceived by Brian Copland in 1950s, substituting OSCAR audience data for cruder input originally available to Copland. New model:

$$\text{Cover} = \frac{\text{TAM}}{\text{TAM} + 1.16\text{T} + 2.84} \, (\times 100 = \% \text{ cover})$$

T is the number of weeks in campaign, M is millions of OTS per week, and A is a measure of exposure to roadside poster medium. Average frequency (F) is given by the expression TAM + 1.16T + 2.84.

copy. 1. All material to be printed, both text and illustrations. 2. From an editorial point of view, the text. 3. A single 'copy' of a publication. 4. In advertising, the text as produced by the copywriter.

copy date. Publisher's deadline for advertisement copy.

Copy Panel. Assists Committee of Advertising Practice. Members are drawn from the Committee's sponsoring organisations who are widely experienced in creating and assessing advertisements. Panel is divided into five groups, one of which is available each week to deal, either before or after publication, with any problem on interpretation of the BCAP.

copy platform. Theme of advertising campaign.

copy point recall. Advertisement recall research which tests recall of advertisement content. This can indicate any need to modify advertisement in order to achieve better recall. Advocates of TRACKING STUDIES consider this inadequate.

copy prep. Instructions written on copy for typesetter to follow.

copy testing. Form of advertisement research to test response to alternative versions of advertisement. FOLDER TECHNIQUE often used to test press ads. TV commercials tested IN-THEATRE. A/B SPLIT METHOD and other split run research is used.

copyfitting. Specifying type to fit space.

copyright. According to COPYRIGHT, DESIGNS AND PATENTS ACT 1988 copyright is a property right which subsists . . . in the following descriptions of work—(a) original literary, dramatic, musical or artistic works, (b) sound recordings, films, broadcasts or cable programmes, and (c) the typographical arrangement of published editions. Copyright does not subsist in a work unless the qualification requirements are satisfied as regards—(a) the author, (b) the country in which the work was first published or (c) in the case of a broadcast or cable programme, the country from which the broadcast was made or the cable programme was sent. Normally, the duration of copyright is for 50 years from the calendar year in which the author dies, film is released, broadcast is made or is included in a cable programme.

Copyright, Designs and Patents Act 1988. Restated law of copyright as set out in the Copyright Act 1956; made fresh

COPYRIGHT, INFRINGEMENT OF

provisions as to the rights of performers and others in performances; conferred a design right in original designs; amended
Registered Designs Act 1949; made provision with respect to
patent agents and trade mark agents; conferred patents and
designs jurisdiction on certain county courts; amended law
of patents; made provision with respect to devices designed
to circumvent copy-protection of works in electronic form;
made fresh provisions penalising the fraudulent reception of
transmissions; and made the fraudulent application or use of
a trade mark an offence. Copyright does not subsist in a literary, dramatic or musical work unless and until it is recorded,
in writing or otherwise.

See ARTISTIC WORK; ARTISTIC WORKS, ADVERTISING OF; BROAD-
CAST; CABLE PROGRAMME; COPYRIGHT; COPYRIGHT INFRINGE-
MENT; COPYRIGHT OWNERSHIP; DEROGATORY TREATMENT;
DESIGN; DESIGN DOCUMENTS; DESIGN RIGHT; DRAMATIC WORK;
FILM; GRAPHIC WORK; ILLICIT RECORDING; LITERARY WORK;
MORAL RIGHTS; PERFORMERS, RIGHTS OF; PHOTOGRAPH; PRIVACY
IN PHOTOGRAPHS, FILMS; SOUND RECORDING; TRADE MARK, FRAU-
DULENT USE OF.

copyright, infringement of. The COPYRIGHT, DESIGNS AND
PATENTS ACT 1988 lays down specific rules regarding acts restricted by copyright in a work and infringement of copyright
by copying. Copying includes storing the work in any medium
by electronic means. It also concerns the issue to the public
of copies, or public performance, e.g. in a public lecture, or
by any mode of visual or acoustic presentation by means of
a sound recording, film, broadcast or cable programme of the
work. There are substantial sub-sections on these matters in
the Act. However, there is relaxation of the regulations when
copyright material is used for research, private study, criticism,
review, news reporting and for educational purposes and where
there is fair dealing in such usage. Librarians may copy material for purposes of research or private study.

A typical example of permissable use of copyright material

lies in Section 30 of the Act which says: 'Fair dealing with a work for the purpose of review or criticism, of that or another work or of a performance of a work, does not infringe any copyright in the work provided that it is accompanied by a sufficient acknowledgement.' (This quotation is an example, as are others in this dictionary concerning the Act, or BCAP or other sources of quotations).

Similarly, educational establishments are permitted to record broadcast or cable programmes, e.g. a video recording. Legal action may be taken against infringement, and a court may order for delivery up to copyright owner of infringing copy or article, and a court may seize infringing copies and other articles if exposed or available for sale or hire.

copyright ownership. According to the COPYRIGHT, DESIGNS AND PATENTS ACT 1988, first ownership of copyright is as follows: (1) The author of a work is the first owner of any copyright in it, subject to the following provisions. (2) Where a literary, dramatic, musical or artistic work is made by an employee in the course of his employment, his employer is the first owner of any copyright in the work subject to any agreement to the contrary. This does not apply to Crown or Parliamentary copyright or that of certain international organisations.

copywriter. Person who writes the text or copy for an advertisement, usually conceiving a theme or copy platform. He may work in agency under a copy chief or in a creative group, in in-house advertising department, or as freelance.

corporate identity. Visual and physical representation of an organisation by means of livery of its vehicles, aircraft, ships; logo, typography, colour schemes; dress, uniform, badge; facia boards, name displays, flags; and other items such as ashtrays, ties, cuff-links, tableware. Not to be confused with CORPORATE IMAGE.

corporate image. Perceived mental impression of an organisation based on knowledge and experience. Everyone's corporate image will therefore vary according to their knowledge and experience of an organisation.

corrected overlay. Translucent overlay, registered on art work, on which corrections are made.

corrective advertising. Advertising which the advertiser is obliged to insert when Advertising Standards Authority has ruled that an ad had offended against BCAP. This has happened with knocking copy motor-car advertisements.

corrigenda. List of corrected printing errors.

cost-per-order. Extension of cost-per-reply (*see* KEY) to cost of conversion of enquiry into business, or cost of getting an order from direct response advertising. Depends as much on targeting as on the direct mail shot or off-the-page advertisement. The use of life-style lists and geodemographic location systems, e.g. ACORN etc, can reduce cost-per-order.

cost-per-reply. *See* KEY.

cost per thousand. Can apply to broadcast media audience figures or press circulation or readership figures. With commercial radio (ILR) 'cost per thousand' is the basic term to express the radio's unit cost. Most frequently used to compare the cost of 1,000 IMPACTS on different stations, it is also used to compare the cost of reaching 1,000 people on the different media.

$$\frac{\text{Schedule Cost}}{\text{Impacts (in 000's)}} = \text{Cost per thousand}$$

Council of Europe Convention on Broadcasting. Lays down directives on European broadcasting including Article 14 on advertising. Article 7 refers to acceptable commercial breaks.

counter. Centre of a type character enclosed by strokes.

coupon. Means of obtaining response to an advertisement, either enquiries or orders. Should be positioned at edge of advertisement for easy clipping, which can be encouraged by dot line and scissor symbols. Can have a KEY to identify origin.

COVER

It should state clearly what is being offered or sold. If there are alternatives, boxes can be printed to be ticked for choice. If payment by instalments is offered, total price must be shown. If payment may be made by credit cards, the ones accepted can be illustrated. Essential that adequate space is given for full name, address, and post code.

cover. Number of times advertisement is read, seen or heard. Gross cover is the total volume of cover. Net cover is the percentage of target audience who get at least one exposure. Four plus cover is the percentage receiving at least four exposures. *See* CUMULATIVE COVER.

cover and frequency analysis. Provided by OSCAR. Supplies data on 110,000 OSCAR assessed panels owned by OAA members. Developed under auspices of JICPAR representing all sides of advertising industry. Makes outdoor a plannable medium, quantifying actual/potential contact with target audiences, nationally/regionally. Uses new COPLAND MODEL. Offers regional target groups (ten ISBA regions or combined regions, London, other conurbations, all conurbations), men, women, 15-44, 45 + ; ABC^1, C^2DE, age and sex, social grades and sex. National target groups as above in greater detail, plus working status, household size, terminal education age, weight of viewing by sex, age, social grade, listening, readership of individual titles, frequency of reading grouped titles.

cover date. Publication date printed on the cover of a publication.

cover price. Retail selling price of a publication printed on the cover. Some magazines have high cover prices to produce revenue when advertisement revenue low. Few publications subsidised by advertisements and cover price, even of popular newspapers, has to contribute to revenue. More recently, Saturday/Sunday newspapers increased cover prices to pay for weekend magazines.

coverage (TV). Percentage of potential audience exposed to television advertising. Can relate to those exposed to an individual television spot, or to at least one of a campaign's television spots. Net coverage or REACH.

CPO. *See* COST-PER-ORDER.

CPT. *See* COST PER THOUSAND.

creative boutique. Another name for an A LA CARTE ADVERTISING AGENCY.

creative group. In large advertising agency, group of executives comprising TV producer, copywriter, visualiser, TV storyboard artist who will work as a team on major accounts.

Creative Handbook. Full-colour pictorial directory of design and graphics, illustration, photography, photographic services, print, film and video, sound, audio visual, supplies and equipment, advertising and other agencies, etc. Annual, British Media Publications, East Grinstead, West Sussex.

crinklies. *See* WRINKLIES.

cromalin. Substitute for ordinary four-colour print.

Croner's Europe. Compendium on single European market. 1989. Covers drafting commercial agreements, intellectual property rights, consumer protection, trading and marketing to the single market, etc. Croner Publications, New Malden, Surrey.

cross-border direct mail. Mailshots mailed from one country to another, with problems of offending against regulations in the recipient's country. The DIRECT MAIL SERVICES STANDARDS BOARD has sought joint agreements to prevent, for instance, financial mailings from European countries which do not conform with the Financial Services Act.

cross-branding promotion. SALES PROMOTION scheme when one manufacturer makes promotional offer of another manufacturer's product on the packing.

cross-couponing. SALES PROMOTION scheme in which purchasers of one product are offered special offer of another product, usually another brand by same manufacturer. Helps promote slower lines or introduce a new one.

cross-hatch. Shading a drawing with criss-crossing parallel lines.

cross-selling. Selling additional lines to existing customers, as in DIRECT RESPONSE marketing.

cross track 16-sheet. Poster site on the wall facing the platform on London Underground. 12ft away from waiting passengers.

crossover test. Testing alternative advertisements by running each in two different journals, and then swapping them over in the next editions, and measuring response to each advertisement in each journal. Suitable for couponed advertisements and especially for direct response OFF-THE-PAGE advertisements.

crumblies. *See* WRINKLIES.

cumulative audience. Number of different people listening to radio during a specified period of time. The potential group that can be exposed to advertising on radio station, and is usually expressed in actual numbers and as a percentage of the population or demographic group.

cumulative cover. Build-up of readership as series of press ads appear.

cure. No advertisement should employ words, phrases or illustrations which claim or imply the cure of any ailment, illness or disease, as distinct from the relief of its symptoms, Part C, Section 5.1, BRITISH CODE OF ADVERTISING PRACTICE.

cursives. Typefaces resembling handwriting, but without joined characters.

custom playing cards. *See* PLAYING CARDS, TUCKBOXES.

customer-get-customer. In DIRECT RESPONSE marketing, the customer is offered a gift for recruiting a new one.

customer profile. Structure of consumer population breakdown of age, sex, social grade, marital status, geographical distribution and shopping habits.

customer segmentation model. As applied to the creation of a database, identifies high, medium and low volume users. Mix of variables may include: value of business; volume of business; industry sector; geographic location; length of relationship; products purchased; credit history; new business potential. Useful when compiling database for direct response marketing.

customer service. Vital part of after-market, dealing with queries, complaints; providing spare parts and repair service; instruction leaflets and manuals; guarantees and promises; and any other service relevant to product.

cut screen dots. When screen tints and halftones are created digitally instead of by older metal plate method, the screen dots can be divided pixel by pixel. The smallest reproduceable unit is therefore not the screen dot but the smallest exposable point—the pixel—of the laser imagesetter. Dot cutting produces improved image definition, especially of line art.

cutting copy. First version of a TV commercial before complete POST PRODUCTION or final editing.

cyan. In four-colour printing, standard shade of blue.

cycle of advertising development. (i) moving strategy definition—what to say and to whom; (ii) creative development—how to say it; (iii) communication assessment—have we said it?; and (iv) campaign evaluation—what was the effect of what we said?

D

damper. On litho printing machine, roller which moistens the printing plate before inking. This carries out the litho principle that grease and water do not mix, thus removing surplus ink from printing image.

dandy roll. On papermaking machine, the cylinder which creates watermarks.

Data Protection Act 1986. Makes it an offence to hold personal data without being registered as a data user unless entitled to exemption. Covers any type of personal information held on a computer. Members of public may apply for print outs of data concerning themselves, usually at fee of about £10. However, the problem can be to know who holds data and on which of their files it is held.

Data Protection Committee. Committee of the ADVERTISING ASSOCIATION representing all industries using databases. Contested interpretation of Note 19 from Data Protection Registrar which implied that database users such as direct marketers and advertising agencies should notify data subjects of proposed use of their names.

Data Protection Register. Lists registered holders of personal computer data. Copies of the Register are held in public libraries for access by members of the public.

Data Protection Tribunal. Tribunal to which data users may appeal against enforcement or de-registration notices under DATA PROTECTION ACT.

database. In DIRECT MAIL, a computerised MAILING LIST, usually based on information originally recorded of, for instance, customers, donors or members. Print outs of labels are available for direct mail purposes.

database marketing. Sophisticated use of database information for DIRECT RESPONSE marketing. In addition to HOLDING MAILING

LIST data, sales leads can be generated, prospects can be tracked, effectiveness of lead sources can be analysed, future sales can be forecast, and budget can be controlled. It is thus not merely a means of addressing prospects but of being informed about their buying characteristics. *See* CUSTOMER SEGMENTATION MODEL.

dataset. Software to send or receive keyboarded data or COPY from word processors to a computerised typesetter by telephone without need to re-keyboard. Saves time and errors, and makes proofing quicker.

date-plan. Plan which states when and where advertisements will appear.

day after recall. Advertisement research method to measure recall of advertisements seen or heard on previous day. *See* AIDED RECALL, TRACKING STUDIES.

Day Glow. Proprietary name for fluorescent inks used for printing posters.

day-part. Segments of day for TV advertising, e.g. DAYTIME, pre-peak, peak-time, post-peak. *See* PEAK LISTENING HOURS (radio), PEAK VIEWING HOURS (TV).

daytime. With TV advertising, usually before 4pm on weekdays.

DBS. *See* DIRECT BROADCASTING BY SATELLITE.

dc. double column. Twice width of newspaper column. Written in lower case.

DC. Double crown. Poster size. Written in caps.

dealer, retail or store audit. Continuous research using panel of shops. Invoices, stocks audited monthly by representative of research company, to produce shares of market held by brands. A.C. Nielsen & Co. Ltd and other research firms conduct shop audits and publish reports or Indices. Covers consumer sales by packages, weights etc; consumer sales sterling value; retail purchases; source of purchase; retailer stocks, stock cover; average stocks per shop handling; average monthly sales—per shop handling; average retail selling price; distribution—shop basis; distribution and annual all-commodity basis; display distribution—shop basis; display distribution—money basis. *See* NIELSEN SCANTRACK.

dealer loader. In SALES PROMOTION, a gift or premium offer to a dealer after he has displayed it during a sales promotion scheme.

decalcomania. Transparency or transparent gelatinous film bearing advertisement that is fixed to a shop window.

deccies. PSYCHOGRAPHIC type, people who are obsessively interested in decorating their houses.

deck panels. Outdoor advertising panels built one above the other.

de-duplicate. Deletion of repeated names from MAILING LIST. This depends on a name being repeated in a similar form which can be detected. Not easy to find misspelt duplicates. Accuracy will depend on original keying of names. *See* PROBABILITY RANKING.

de-massification. Fractionalisation. Breakdown of conventional mass-market media to that which appeals to special audiences or readerships, as described by TOFFLER, ALVIN. Already seen with emergence of economically viable newspapers with modest circulations, and greater choice of TV channels as provided by cable and satellite TV, but it is slow to succeed with British newspapers. Exceptions are *Today* (with change of ownership) and *The Independent*. In contrast, in 1986–88 new newspapers such as: *Sunday Today, London Daily News, Evening News (London), News On Sunday, North-West Times* and *The Post* all failed.

definition. In a photograph or its reproduction, quality of detail and sharpness.

demographic market profile. Age, sex, social grade, geographical distribution and so on.

demographic targeting. Directing advertising at certain sections of the public. Publications have their DEMOGRAPHIC PROFILES. Direct mail can be aimed at geodemographic audiences using ACORN, MOSAIC, PIN, SUPER PROFILES.

demographics. Selection of people according to age, sex, income, occupation, geographical distribution and special interests and possessions. Means of segmenting consumer market. Research organisations like AGB have data bank for categorising.

demography. Study of population and its characteristics, based on census returns.

denigration. Otherwise known as ASHCANNING or knocking copy, general rules 22.1–22.3 of the British Code of Advertising Practice deal with denigration. These rules state that advertisers should not seek to discredit products of their competitors by unfair means; no advertisement should contain inaccurate or irrelevant comments on the person, character or actions of a competitor; nor should any advertisement describe or show the products of a competitor as broken or defaced, inoperative or ineffective.

densitometer. Instrument for measuring tonal value of photographic or printed area.

density. Tonal value of a photographic or printed area.

deprivation question. In group depth interviewing, the question which asks respondents which product they would miss most if it were no longer available.

depth interview or focussed interview. In marketing research, an interview based on open-ended questions instead of a STRUCTURED QUESTIONNAIRE. *See also* FREE INTERVIEW, FUNNEL TECHNIQUE. Interviewer makes a written summary of all answers.

derogatory treatment. Section 80 of Chapter IV (Moral Rights) of the COPYRIGHT, DESIGNS AND PATENTS ACT 1988 protects the author of a copyright literary, dramatic, musical or artistic work against derogatory treatment of his work. This treatment can apply to any addition to, deletion from, alteration to or adaptation of the work, other than a translation or minor arrangement or transcription of a musical work. Treatment is derogatory if it amounts to distortion or mutilation of the work or is otherwise prejudicial to the honour or reputation of the author or director.

descender. Lower part or stroke of lower case letters such as j, p, q or y.

design. According to the COPYRIGHT, DESIGNS AND PATENTS ACT 1988, Section 213(2), design means the design of any aspect of the shape or configuration (whether internal or external) of the whole part of an article. NB, this differs from the definition of REGISTERED DESIGNS in Section 265.

design document. According to the COPYRIGHT, DESIGNS AND PATENTS ACT 1988, design document means any record of a design, whether in the form of a drawing, a written description, a photograph, data stored in a computer or otherwise.

design right. *See* DESIGN. (i) The designer is the first owner of any design right in a design which is not created in pursuance of a commission or in the course of employment. (ii) Where a design is created in pursuance of a commission, the person commissioning the design is the first owner of any design right in it. (iii) Where, in a case not falling within subsection (ii) a design is created by an employee in the course of his employment, his employer is the first owner of any design right in the design. These three paragraphs appear in Section 215 of the Copyright, Designs and Patents Act 1988. 216-(1) Design right expires (a) 15 years from the end of the calendar year in which the design was first recorded in a DESIGN DOCUMENT or an article was first made to the design, whichever first occurred, or (b) if articles made to the design are made available for sale or hire within five years from the end of that calendar year, ten years from the end of the calendar year in which that first occurred.

Design Week. Weekly magazine for the design industry. 1988. London.

Designers and Art Directors' Association Awards. Annual DADA awards for best graphic, advertising, TV and editorial work.

desktop media. Direct media sent to executives at home. *See also* DOORMAT MEDIA.

desktop publishing. Creation of house journals, commercial journals and other print by means of a personal computer which handles copy, editing, setting and layout. Typical systems used are Apple Mackintosh, Pagemaker. Computer-aided publishing.

diacriticals. Accent marks found in foreign languages such as marks or signs above or below letters of the alphabet.

diaresis. Two dots over a vowel as in umlauts ö and ü.

diorama. Three-dimensional scenic illustrated point-of-sale display, or miniature set used in TV studio to simulate life-size location.

Diatronic. Superb quality digital type produced by Berthold Diatronic machines. Letter forms produced at Berthold produce faultless image. These typefaces are then laid down in negative form on high quality glass matrices. By utilising prisms and mirrors light is passed through the negative character to the photographic material. The resultant matchless image has created the industry standard known as Diatronic quality.

Diazo. Copying process, e.g. blue print, using light sensitive compounds (diazonnium).

dichotomous question. As used in a questionnaire when there is only a yes or no answer.

didone. 'Modern' typefaces with vertical sides or thicknesses to letters such as 'o', as distinct from old-style faces with sloping sides.

die-cut. Print or display piece cut to special shape with knife-edge die. Used in mailshots and sales literature to produce windows and POP-UPS.

die-stamping. Intaglio printing process giving relief impression, made with male and female steel dies. Used for quality letterheadings.

Digest of Brands and Advertisers. Quarterly digest from MEAL. Shows combined TV, radio, press expenditure of individual brands during latest quarter; each month in quarter and preceding 12 months. It also shows the split between three media for each brand and product group during latest 12-month period. On-line Access: results of Digest available via Market Analysis and Information Database (MAID); profile Information (MAGIC); and Finsbury Data Services (Textline).

Digital Design. 1988. Bernard Holthusen's graphic reference book to aid designers in the preparation of work which will be produced on the latest generation of electronic graphic systems. Lavishly illustrated. Chapters on type, type and screens, rules and screens, graphic shapes, line art, halftone pictures, European process colour scale, real colours and process colours, typesetting examples, bookwork typefaces. Printed in English, German, French. Published by ECON Verlag, Dusseldorf. In UK: Scangraphic Visutek Ltd, Leatherhead, Surrey.

digital typesetting. Computerised typesetting whereby a character is held in a computer in a digital format. This information is sent to the laser recorder. The laser beam is then instructed to turn on and off, building up the pre-defined shapes with a series of spots of light, and so exposing the photographic material. Digital technology makes it possible to produce complete made-up jobs. This process allows a flexibility to be able to modify characters, reverse them out of black or tinted areas, or rotate type to varying angles, to produce a single piece of artwork for an advertisement or piece of print. Typesetters such as Impact Typesetting Ltd, Birmingham, use high definition Diamond types. An outline shape is pre-defined on an

Ikarus computer, and the laser beam then fills the shape with either black or tinted areas. These Diamond types have DIATRONIC quality. *See* OPTO-MECHANICAL TYPESETTING, SCANTEX 2000.

Dinkie. Acronym for PSYCHOGRAPHIC TYPE, 'double income no kids' married couple.

DipCAM. *See* COMMUNICATION, ADVERTISING AND MARKETING EDUCATION FOUNDATION.

direct advertising. *See* HOUSE-TO-HOUSE DISTRIBUTION.

Direct Broadcasting by Satellite. Broadcasting of TV programmes direct to homes via a dish aerial measuring between 35cm and 85cm acccording to power of the satellite and geographical location of the home. Differs from low power distribution satellites which need large dish. SKY CHANNEL and British Satellite Broadcasting use DBS system. *See also* SATELLITE TELEVISION. ASTRA, used by Sky Channel, is a 16-channel medium-power pan-European satellite and is received on home dishes of 60cm to 90cm diameter.

direct input. Keying in editorial material in computerised newsroom, and replacing hot metal foundry in newspaper print shop, sub-editing and page layout also computerised.

direct litho. Unlike OFFSET LITHO, printing process which transfers an image direct from plate to paper without first printing the reversed image to a blanket and offsetting it to paper. Used for printing magazine covers.

direct mail. Britain's third largest advertising medium using mailing lists or databases and postal services. One of the main media of DIRECT RESPONSE marketing. *See* BDMA, FORTY-FORTY-TWENTY RULE, JUNK MAIL, MAILING PREFERENCE SERVICE.

Direct Mail Producers' Association. Represents production side of direct mail industry. Has its own code of practice. London.

Direct Mail Services Standards Board. 1983. Runs a recognition system for direct mail agencies which adhere to BCAP and other codes. London.

direct marketing. *See* DIRECT RESPONSE.

direct response. Modern name for mail order, using DIRECT MAIL, catalogues, MAIL DROPS, OFF-THE-PAGE press ads, TV, telemarketing. Also called direct marketing.

Direct Response. Controlled circulation monthly journal of direct response marketing. Hertford. 1980.

Direct Response Advertising Yearbook. Records statistical intelligence relating exclusively to couponed space and insert advertising. Annual. Nationwide Market Research Ltd, Basingstoke, Hants.

dirty copy, proof. Opposite to clean copy or proof. Original copy containing many handwritten amendments, or proof requiring many corrections.

disaggregated data. From individual research returns, such as diaries from panelists, effect of advertising on purchases can be identified.

discretionary income. Extra income over and above that required to cover basic needs. Advertising for luxuries competes for available discretionary income.

discrimination test. Research test which shows how many people can differentiate between products being tested. *See* TRIADIC TEST.

discussion group. Modified form of MOTIVATIONAL RESEARCH. Recruited group gives spontaneous answers to questions from chairman. Works best if members have a common interest. Can be too small to be representative. Possibility of bias by group leader. But can be effective and is inexpensive.

dispenser. Display device used on counters for leaflets.

display outer. Carton for small unit goods which can be converted into a dispenser with a display panel which folds out of lid. Useful for counter and shelf displays.

display type. Large, bold and often decorative type used for headlines and subheadings in contrast to small text type.

displayed advertisement. Opposite to a run-on classified ad, in which various type faces and sizes and sometimes illustrations are used.

displayed classified. DISPLAYED ADVERTISEMENT placed in the classified columns of a publication.

dissolve. *See* OPTICALS.

doctor blade. In PHOTOGRAVURE and FLEXOGRAPHY printing, a blade which removes excess ink from printing plate.

doggerel. Light, often amusing and usually irregular verse sometimes used in advertisement copy.

door-to-door distribution. Direct advertising material delivered door-to-door. There are specialist distributors, the Post Office Household Delivery Service, and distribution with FREE NEWSPAPERS. Can be TARGETED using geodemographic systems as with DEMOGRAPHIC TARGETING like ACORN.

doormat media. Direct mail addressed to consumer at home. *See also* DESKTOP MEDIA.

doorstopper milk bottles. Advertising printed on milk bottles, said to each make average of 24 journeys. Used by confectionery firms. A national campaign could reach 17 million homes and possibly 36 million adults.

double-barrelled question. A question to avoid in a research questionnaire since it poses two questions simultaneously, neither of which may be answered adequately.

double fronts, rears. Pairs of double crown posters on front or back of upper deck of double-decker bus.

double-head. In production of a television commercial when sound and vision are still on separate tapes. *See* MARRIED PRINT.

double-placement. Form of product pre-testing. Existing product A is tested against new product B.

doublespread. Advertisement printed across two pages, either CENTREFOLD SPREAD, or across two facing pages.

downlink. In CABLE TELEVISION, main receiving station or earth station dish which accepts signals from television and also from television and radio frequencies.

downweight factor. When a research technique tends to over-state the market size consistently, a 'downweight' factor is applied to reduce figures in line with 'reality'.

dramatic work. According to the COPYRIGHT, DESIGNS AND PATENTS ACT 1988, a dramatic work includes a work of dance or mime.

drawn-on cover. Method of binding sometimes used for magazines, where the cover is glued to spine of pages.

drip. A regular advertising campaign as distinct from a short-term burst.

drip mat. A coaster, but usually stouter than a paper coaster and made of absorbent board, bearing advertisement, on which customers place drinks in, for example, a pub.

drive and housewife time. Radio advertising term for segments of time when drivers are commuting or, in between, when housewives are at home.

drop initial, capital. First letter of a text set larger than following type and occupying more than one line. Originated from illuminated or decorative drop capitals in handwritten Bibles. Sometimes replaced by setting first word or words in caps, a common newspaper style.

drop out. *See* BLEACH OUT.

dry-brush drawing. One made with a brush and very dry thick ink or paint.

dry transfer lettering. Sheets of characters such as Letraset from which individual letters can be transferred to paper by rubbing. Can replace display typesetting or hand lettering when producing display lines for advertisements or print.

dual channel homes. Homes which qualify as ITV homes for more than one ITV region.

dub. 1. A G-spool. Copy of a video commercial sent to TV stations. 2. To record and add commentary, music, sound, and computer graphics to a film or video. Post production.

dubbing in. Adding one film or video to another, such as adding a commercial to a sponsored show where sponsored tv permitted.

dummy. Booklet of blank pages used when planning a publication or pasting up proofs. Also, a specimen copy of a proposed edition of a newspaper or magazine, used when selling space.

dumper or dump bin. Tub-like POS container to display goods, used to make special offer or attract impulse buyers.

duograph. Printing plate made from black-and-white picture to give two-tone effect, the second printing plate is flat to provide tint. Cheaper than DUOTONE.

duotone. Pair of halftone printing plates made from a one-colour picture to produce a two-colour effect.

duotone pictures. Two-colour pictures, using REAL COLOURS or PROCESS COLOURS. A background colour given a screen angle of 18.4°, and black being printed with a screen angle of 45°. Highlight, midtone and shadow tones of the two colours can be changed to achieve variations. This can be done digitally. *See* SCANTEX 2000.

duplicated readership. Various journals may be read by the same people, which may produce wasteful advertising if the same ad appears in all of them. It is best, therefore, to plan a media schedule with the least amount of duplication, and the greatest reach of different readers.

duplication analysis. Marketing research method of assessing extent of inter-purchasing between brands, sizes or varieties. Can indicate brands with high or low level of inter-purchasing.

dustbin check. Form of CONSUMER PANEL research in which members retain packages which are recorded by interviewer. Plastic sack provided.

E

EAAA. European Association of Advertising Agencies.

EAN code. European article number. *See also* BAR CODING.

ear, ear space or title corner. Front page advertisement space on one or both sides of the title of some newspapers.

early fringe. TV segment before PRIME TIME viewing.

eclectic method. Way of fixing advertising appropriation. *See* COMPOSITE METHOD.

ECU. Extra close up in TV filming.

edit suites. Used for video POST-PRODUCTION with equipment for adding special effects.

editing. 1. In market research, checking that questionnaires are ready for coding and analysis, or that diaries from panelists are free of inconsistencies. There are also computer edit runs to check data against criteria. 2. In film and video making, editing raw film or tape to delete, add or change sequence. Editing can tighten up action and bring finished film or tape to desired length.

edition binding. In book production, method of binding SIGNA-TURES of 16 or 32 pages, sewing them together and then glueing them to the book back before binding them into covers.

EDMA. *See* EUROPEAN DIRECT MARKETING ASSOCIATION.

educational promotion. SALES PROMOTION scheme with an edu-cational or cultural appeal to children.

egocentric arrogance. Advertising which carries no brand name or logo yet succeeds in being identified, e.g. Silk Cut cigarette posters showing a piece of silk with a cut in it.

Egyptian. Slab serif typeface like Rockwell, Cairo, Karnak which have SERIFS and strokes of the same thickness.

elaboration likelihood model. Research model for explaining consumer involvement in response to advertising. If elaboration likelihood is high, more informative advertising is justified but if it is low, more simple, repetitive advertising is necessary.

elasticity method. Method of fixing advertising appropriation on basis of supply and demand curves. The average cost of an extra unit of expenditure on advertising is compared with average return on higher profit. This shows the point beyond which further advertising is uneconomic.

electric spectaculars. Outdoor advertisements consisting of words or designs made up with electric lights.

electronic media. Newscaster, radio or television media.

electronic page. Teletext page or pages held on PRESTEL or ORACLE computer and available to viewers with teletext receivers. Prestel is available via telephone system, with charges for calling up pages, Oracle is on air direct to the TV set with no charges.

electronic point-of-sale systems. Reads EAN bar codes on packages so that a check-out assistant can print the till receipt and charge the customer. Also records stock movement and aids stock control.

electronic publishing. *See* DESKTOP PUBLISHING.

electronic retouching. Unlike conventional hand retouching, halftone retouching by digital techniques allows direct manipulation of all grey values with exceptional level of quality and precision. Tone values can be generated in a more or less stepless range, and parts of pictures can be transplanted so that changes can be made to complex course tone areas. This is useful when retouching skin tones, or for cut-out and montage functions. Can avoid hard edges to contours of cut-out pictures on white backgrounds. *See* SCANTEX 2000.

electronic scanner. Means of scanning full-colour copy wrapped round drums by reading colour densities and producing colour separations. Also transmits control readings on printing press or paper making machine.

ellipsis. Three dots are printed when words are omitted. In copywriting this is a means of reducing the number of words and speeding up the reading.

em. Square of a given size of type, usually 12 points, used as a unit of measurement for lines, columns or type areas.

embossing. Printing a name, design or logo so that it has a raised surface. *See also* FOIL STAMPING.

emphasis, law of. Dependence of emphasis on contrast, such as bold headline and lighter weight text type, or use of white space.

emphatic full point. Use of full point or full stop to give emphasis, such as by punctuating headline of an advertisement.

empty nesters. Couples without children. *See* PSYCHOGRAPHIC TYPES.

en. Unit of measurement, half of the EM space in width but the same in depth.

end aisle. In supermarkets, premium display space where products may be stacked on floor instead of being given limited shelf space.

end-product advertising. Advertising which promotes raw materials, ingredients, components or accessories to the makers of finished product. *See* BACK SELLING.

endorser potential. Qualities of a celebrity as an endorser of products in advertising. Can vanish if the celebrity is involved in scandal.

enumeration district. Smallest unit for which there are census figures. 125,000 in Britain. Average population 460.

envelopes. *See* BANGTAIL, POLYTHENE MAILERS.

EP. *See* ELECTRONIC PUBLISHING.

Epica Awards. European creative advertising awards. Supported by the Commission of the European Communities and the European Association of Advertising Agencies. Entries are judged by 20 advertising journals from 13 countries. The award is sponsored by AVNET, the electronic outdoor media. Winning entries and other outstanding campaigns are published in annual Epica Book. Epica, 5 rue Talma, 75016 Paris, France.

EPOS. *See* ELECTRONIC POINT-OF-SALE SYSTEMS.

equal impacts. Setting of rating points for each TV region to get balanced overall coverage in a networked campaign.

Equity. Actors' trade union which negotiates rates for actors appearing in television and radio commercials.

escalator panel. Advertisement panel on the wall of escalator shaft, as in London Underground.

ESOMAR. *See* EUROPEAN SOCIETY FOR MARKET AND OPINION RESEARCH.

ESTBC. *See* EUROPEAN SATELLITE TELEVISION BROADCASTING CORPORATION.

ethical pharmaceuticals. Pharmaceuticals distributed to hospital pharmacists and to chemists for making up doctor's prescriptions. Usually branded, but not sold to public like OVER THE COUNTER proprietary medicines.

ethnic community radio. Among the first ethnic community radio stations the IBA awarded contracts in 1989 for Hounslow, Haringey, Brixton and a bigger one for Greater London. Programmes are mostly in English and some six Asian languages but they may include other languages as Greater London has many ethnic groups.

ethnic media. There are some 60 ethnic magazines and newspapers published in the UK, mostly addressed to Asians in their languages, or to West Indians. *See also* ETHNIC COMMUNITY RADIO.

Euro-branding. Choosing BRAND names for products sold throughout Europe (and especially in the Single European Market). Names must be acceptable whatever the language and not suffer from double or unfortunate meanings in other languages. Very important when advertising by cross-frontier SATELLITE TV.

Euromarketing. Weekly European marketing news bulletin, published by *Advertising Age*. London.

European Advertising Tripartite. Represents combined interests of advertisers, agencies and media at European Community level. It shares secretarial facilities with European Association of Advertising Associations, European Association of Advertising Agencies, Communauté des Associations des Editeurs des Journaux de la CEE (Federation of Associations of Periodical Publishers in the EEC), European Group of Television Advertising, and the Advertising Information Group.

European Association of Advertising Agencies. Trade association of European advertising agencies. *See* EUROPEAN ADVERTISING TRIPARTITE.

European Business Channel. Zurich-based TV service linked to German-(RTL +) and English-language (Sky Channel) television networks. It began transmission November 1988 and was delivered by cable TV. Mostly breakfast time transmissions to give businessmen briefing for the business day.

European Direct Marketing Association. Promotes direct mail internationally. Acts as international forum sales platform. Annual awards for direct marketing campaigns. It is based at Kempratin SG, Switzerland.

European process colour scale. Din 16539. Consists of cyan, magenta, yellow and black.

European Satellite Television Broadcasting Corporation. Five-nation European TV consortium.

European Society for Market and Opinion Research. Holds annual conference in major European city when important papers are presented. Amsterdam.

Eutelsat IFI. Multi-channel satellite including Sky, Super Channel, French TV.

even small caps. Small capital letters without full-size initial caps.

executive gifts. Advertising gifts, such as diaries, pens, wines and spirits, presented to clients, especially at Christmas, but also at visits and events. May be made specially as company souvenirs such as models, paper weights, etc. But of higher quality than promotional give-aways.

Exhibition Bulletin. Gives information about forthcoming shows home and overseas. Monthly. The London Bureau, Sydenham. 1948.

exhibition train. One which can be toured to a number of towns where it will remain at the station for a few days and be visited by invited guests.

expanded. Broad, extended version of a typeface.

exploded drawing. One which reveals interior of a subject which would not be visible from a photograph. Usually open line drawing.

exposure. Total number of viewers, listeners, readers or visitors, to which an advertisement may be exposed according to the medium.

exposure/impacts (TV). *See* TELEVISION RATING (TVR).

ext. Extended type characters.

extended group discussion. Complex qualitative motivational group discussion running for some hours, and using methods such as role-playing, analogies, or story completion, revealing spontaneous unconscious ideas, which can be incorporated.

extra. Actor who plays minor role in TV commercial and does not earn repeat fees.

extra-fill, weight packs. SALES PROMOTION packs which contain, for instance, '10% extra' at no extra charge.

extra origination charges. Those made by publishers for four-colour artwork requiring more than one transparency.

eyeblink test. Using a hidden camera, the eyeblink rate of respondents is recorded to measure extent of emotional tension provoked by a TV commercial being tested.

eyepath. In layout or picture, a composition which directs the eye to the starting point of the design.

F

face. 1. A design of typeface such as Plantin, Rockwell or Univers. 2. Printing surface of a piece of metal type.

face sheet data. In a research questionnaire, the respondent's personal details.

face-to-face interviewing. In marketing research, street, doorstep or in-home interviewing as distinct from postal or telephone enquiries.

facilities house. Video producer who supplies packaged TV elements such as programme titles, trailers, station identifications and promotional fillers.

facing, next matter. Press advertisement space next to editorial material.

facings. Sides of packs which can be seen on shop shelves.

facsimile pages. In newspaper production. Pages completed on screen in editorial offices and transmitted by fax to the press at another location or to a regional contract printer. *Daily Mail* faxes pages from Kensington to Rotherhithe.

facts book. 1. File of contact reports made by agency account executive. 2. Details about a product held by a BRAND or PRODUCT MANAGER.

Facts of Living Survey. Conducted by ICD Direct, lifestyle questionnaire distributed to 15m consumers. The questions deal with leisure interests, health and fitness, hobbies, readership of magazines/newspapers, holidays, motoring, home maintenance, finance and personal data. Respondents are offered a prize draw and discount vouchers and offers. Companies subscribe by including their own questions in omnibus survey type questionnaire. *See* LIFESTYLE SURVEY.

fair copy. Copy free of printing errors.

Fair Trading Act 1973. The Act appoints a Director-General of Fair Trading, and staff, to study the effect upon consumers' interests of trading practices and commercial activities of every kind and to recommend government action where necessary. *See* OFFICE OF FAIR TRADING; COMMISSION SYSTEM; MAIL ORDER TRANSACTIONS (INFORMATION ORDER) 1976.

family. Variations of a typeface by weight, widths or design such as light, medium, bold, extra bold, condensed, expanded, roman, italic, shadow.

fast-moving consumer goods. fmcgs. Small unit repeat-purchase goods, typical of those stocked by supermarkets.

fat face. Typeface with extra thick contrasting strokes.

fax mailing. Direct mail by facsimile machine and use of fax numbers. Permits space of an off-the-page press advertisement. Has largely replaced similar mailings by telex.

fear and distress. The British Code of Advertising is specific in ruling against appeals to fear, both in general advertising (e.g. for insurance) or in health claims for medical products. In Part B, Section 15.1 the code states that, without good reason, no advertisement should play on fear or excite distress, while Section 15.2.1 points out that when an appeal to fear is properly made (e.g. to encourage prudent behaviour) the fear evoked should not be disproportionate to the risk addressed. In Part C, 5.4 the Code says no advertisement should cause those who see it unwarranted anxiety lest they are suffering (or may, without responding to the advertiser's offer, suffer) from any disease or condition of health; or suggest that consumption or use of the advertised product is necessary for the maintenance of physical or mental capacities, whether by people in general or by any particular group.

fees, agency. A number of advertising agencies have replaced the anomalous commission system by charging clients net cost of media plus a fee based on time and expertise. This is more professional and the agency can earn income according to the volume and quality of work.

fees, TV presenters. *See* ONE-OFF PAYMENTS, REPEAT FEES.

field research. Marketing research conducted by interviewers in the street, on the doorstep or in the home.

fill-in. In DIRECT MAIL, personal items that have to be added to a letter such as salutation, signature, or personalisation.

filler spots. On ITV, commercials supplied by advertisers which may be shown as air-time permits, and are charged at special low rates.

film. According to the COPYRIGHT, DESIGNS AND PATENTS ACT 1988, film means a recording on any medium from which a moving image may by any means be produced.

film make-up. In printing, positioning FILMSETTINGS or other film ready for platemaking.

film master. Complete film positive of an advertisement from which a plate can be made.

film mechanical. CAMERA-READY COPY in film form instead of paste-up artwork.

filmsetting. Typesetting on film instead of on paper.

filter question. In a marketing research questionnaire, a question which identifies the respondent's relevance to the survey. If the respondent is not relevant, the interview is discontinued.

Fin Pin. Uses the results of 65,000 interviews a year to find, describe and reach customers for financial products and services. Defines people in terms of bank accounts, cash cards, share ownership, mortgages; and identifies neighbourhoods where specific types of people live.

finish. Quality of paper surface, e.g. SUPERCALENDERED. A paper is finished by polishing rollers, not coated.

finished art. Final drawing ready for reproduction.

finished rough. A superior advertisement visual, worked up by studio with colour separations, mechanical artwork and type overlay, for submission to agency client.

first colour down. In printing, the first colour to be printed when there is more than one colour.

first proof. Early proof which is read for literals and printer's errors before submission to client.

first revise. Further proof incorporating corrections.

fishing. Targeting a DIRECT RESPONSE campaign by first seeking prospects by offering free sample to those who return coupon asking about use of a rival product. *See also* MINING, SPELUNKING.

Fix-a-Form labels. Packaging labels with concertina folded leaflets which are released by breaking perforation.

fixed spots. Spot TV commercials transmitted in an agreed break at a special rate. Usually, its subject coincides with that of the programme.

flag. 1. In an outdoor poster, torn paper which hangs loose. 2. Outdoor medium, useful where there are no poster sites, or there is an open area such as a petrol station forecourt.

flagship brand. A manufacturer's best-selling line with which the company is most closely associated, e.g. Heinz baked beans.

flash pack. Specially printed package on which a SALES PROMOTION offer such as a price reduction is 'flashed'.

flashes. Five-second TV slides with voice-over by station announcer.

flat colour. Second colour produced by template or tint.

flat rate. Standard charge for advertisement space or airtime, irrespective of volume or frequency.

flatbed. Printing press with printing image flat on bed of machine, instead of having curved plates as with rotary machines.

flexography. Rotary web LETTERPRESS printing process. Uses flexible rubber plates and fast drying solvent or water-based inks. Used for printing packaging materials, especially delicate ones like foil wrappings. With improved photopolymer plates, inks, rivals offset litho for newspaper printing, and adopted by the *Daily Mail* in 1988. Flexo inks are brighter than offset inks. Good picture reproduction.

floating accents. Accents in a type fount which can be placed above any letter. In digital typesetting, all kinds of accents which are available to make every character combination possible, as when setting foreign names and words, or setting in a foreign language.

fluorescent ink. As used for shop posters, ink which reacts to ultra-violet light and gives glowing effect. *See* DAY GLOW.

fly poster. Poster pasted on site, such as on walls and windows of empty shops without permission, as with pop group/singer posters.

fmcgs. *See* FAST-MOVING CONSUMER GOODS.

focal point interviewing. In marketing research, focussing an interview on a particular theme so that the respondent is encouraged to concentrate on this when responding to questions.

Focoltone. Colour matching system with combination of four process printing colours so that colours can be accurately reproduced as specified by the designer.

focus group. Form of QUALITATIVE RESEARCH. A small group of six to 12 people with common interest is taken. The group leader directs questions and records concensus of answers. Combination of brain-storming and DISCUSSION GROUP techniques.

focussed interview. See DEPTH INTERVIEW.

foil papers. Papers with metallic surfaces, ideal for FLEXO-GRAPHY printing, and used for decorative wrappings.

foil stamping. Means of showing off coins, trademarks, logos by embossing, using heat application of gold or silver inks.

fold-out. Folded sheet which opens out to a larger size, or many times its folded-down size, like a map.

folder technique. Often used in advertisement pre-testing, a number of advertisements being placed in the plastic sleeves of a folder which respondents study in turn before being questioned about what they remember.

foliation. Numbering of pages or folios.

folio. A page or page number.

follow style. In printing, instruction to typesetter to follow the style of a sample print.

font. *See* FOUNT.

footprint. Land area covered by satellite transmission.

force card. In DIE-STAMPING the male die.

fore-edge. Outside edge, opposite the binding edge, of a book.

form. Number of pages printed from one sheet of paper, e.g. in 16s or 32s.

form-mailer. DIRECT MAIL shot comprising a continuous form so designed that the same piece of paper becomes an envelope containing different inserts (reply card, advertisement, etc) all of which create a complete message. Each part can be personalised. Morley-Cox Ltd, Bromley, Kent.

format. Way in which a piece of print is set out, the size and shape of page, e.g. broadsheet newspaper *The Independent* or tabloid *Daily Mirror*, kind of binding, typography. Also, photo-typesetting term for repetitive commands stored as a code, and video format as with Betamax and VHS.

forms close. Copy date when material for printing must be received by publisher.

forty-forty-twenty rule. DIRECT MAIL formula. 40% of success depends on mailing list; 40% on the offer or proposition; 20% on ideas and design.

fount. Complete set of characters to print a particular typeface in one size. The word has two sources of origin: (i) from old French *font*, to melt or cast, (ii) from early days of monastic printing in England when alphabets of printing type were stored in spare founts in the chapel.

fountain. Source of ink supply in printing press.

four-colour process. Full-colour printing using yellow, magenta, cyan and black, whereby the colours of the original artwork are separated by filters.

four plus cover. Percentage of readership or audience who are exposed to an advertisement at least four times.

FP/FC. Full page, full colour.

fractionalisation. *See* DE-MASSIFICATION.

fragrance application. For DIRECT MAIL and SALES PROMOTION purposes, application to print of specially-formulated solution containing micro-encapsulated particles of perfume. When the area is rubbed, fragrance released. Can prompt consumer response. HunterPrint, Corby.

fragrance burst. DIRECT MAIL or SALES PROMOTION process used by cosmetics industry. Perfume fragrance encapsulated between printed sheets so that it 'bursts' out when pulled apart. Hunterprint, Corby.

frame. In cine-film, a single picture. Frames are repeated to create a movie. In Prestel Viewdata, content of TV screen.

frameful. TV screen filled with Prestel information.

free. Said to be most effective word in copywriting. Can be extended to FREEPHONE and FREEPOST.

free-fall insert. Insert tipped into journal.

free interview. Interview based on open-ended questions posed by an interviewer. *See* DEPTH INTERVIEW.

free magazine. In UK, some 300 titles ranging from give-aways on property, jobs, entertainment and religion to MAGALOGUES targeted at up-market readers.

free newspapers. Local newspapers with door-to-door saturation coverage of urban areas. Sometimes four to five competing titles in a large town.

free-standing insert. Loose insert in a newspaper or magazine.

freepak. A5 folder containing 15–20 discount or cash voucher offers, distributed at supermarket checkouts.

Freephone. Facility provided in press advertisements to ring the advertiser free-of-charge. The advertiser pays for call in this case.

Freepost. Means of attracting response by offering post free enquiry or order service. If respondents address an envelope including the word 'Freepost' in the advertiser's address they qualify for second class post. Another possibility is to supply respondents with first or second class reply envelopes using Freepost in address. The user of the service pays a licence fee to Royal Mail Letters, and is charged a handling fee per item, with discounts for bulk items of 50,000 or more a year.

frenchfold. A sheet of print folded into four pages, but exposing only one side which is printed, leaving a join at the edges as with some Christmas cards.

frequency. 1. In publishing, the number of times a newspaper or magazine is published in a given period (e.g. daily, weekly, fortnightly, monthly or quarterly). 2. In broadcasting, the number of cycles per second, stated in hertz, e.g. one kilohertz (kHz).

3. In radio, opportunities to hear. Average number of times the audience reached by an advertising schedule are exposed to a commercial.

$$\frac{\text{Gross impressions (Impacts)}}{\text{Reach}} = \text{Frequency}$$

frequency analysis. Marketing research study which shows how frequently brands are bought. This shows the extent to which a brand depends on few large buyers who make most purchases, rather than on bigger group of less frequent buyers. Reveals percentage of purchasers who buy each brand once, twice, three times in test period.

frequency distribution. Number of people who saw a given number of presentations of an advertisement, especially TV commercials.

fringe time. On TV the hours before (early fringe time) and after (late fringe time) prime time, which may differ between London and regions due to different home-coming from work.

frontier groups. People who represent a new social, political, economic and technological society and resent or are disenchanted with inertia of obsolete or traditional institutions.

fugitive inks. Those which fade quickly and are best avoided in poster printing, e.g. light blue, mauve, pale green.

fulfilment house. Firm which receives the response to MAIL-INS, SALES PROMOTION offers, DIRECT RESPONSE marketing advertisements and despatches what is offered. Handling house.

full-dot screen. Halftone screen consisting of whole dots. With digital production, dots may be round or elliptical. *See* QUARTER-DOT SCREEN.

full-out. Not indented. The first paragraph at the beginning of a text or following a sub-heading is usually not indented. Subsequent paragraphs are indented. book style. Most legible style for TEXT matter.

full-point. Full stop punctuation mark.

full position. In newspaper, NEXT MATTER position or special preferred advertisement.

funnel technique. In marketing research, way of interviewing which directs open-ended question more deliberately than in normal DEPTH INTERVIEW.

G

G-spool. Duplicate copy of a video commercial sent to TV stations.

gable-end. In outdoor advertising, poster site or hoarding on end wall of a building.

Galavision. Pan-European Spanish-language entertainment/ information satellite-to-cable channel, initially aimed at audiences in Spain, Germany and the Netherlands. Launched by giant Mexican Televisa group through Eurovisa of the Netherlands.

galley-proof. First proof before typesetting is imposed or pasted down, usually set solid. Originally from the galley tray in which metal type was placed before being spaced and display lines added.

Gallup Poll. *See* READING AND NOTING TEST.

gang printing. Running more than one printing job on the same sheet.

gatefold. Page in journal which folds out to make extra page or pages. Can also be applied to sales literature and mailshots.

gathering. In printing, collecting and collating pages for binding.

gaze motion. The effect of eyes in illustrations, and how they direct reader's attention. If eyes look in the wrong direction they can distract the reader.

generic brands. Products in plain or 'thrifty' packs, sold loose, or in any way unidentified except as, for instance, 'rice', 'aspirin' or 'soap'.

geodemographic targeting. Reaching required target audiences by means of geographic and demographic classification of residential neighbourhoods. *See* ACORN, DEMOGRAPHIC TARGETING, MOSAIC, PIN and SUPER PROFILES.

Geopin. Geodemographic information running on a desktop computer which will handle any information that can be related to a location, postcode or address. Uses CENTRY database of census information; PiN which analyses 130,000 neighbourhoods into 60 marketing-orientated categories; FiNPiN classification system geared to financial services market; Pinpoint Address Code system of locating individual households; and Pinpoint Road Network database on every kind of thoroughfare. Applicable to door-to-door distribution, postal direct mail, retail direct marketing. System comprises mapping system, area profiling, area ranking, customer profiling, market potential systems, postcode directory and postcode sector boundaries. Pinpoint Analysis Ltd.

get-up. Packaging which distinguishes and identifies a product by its shape, colour, design, typography, logo. *See* PASSING OFF.

GHI. *See* GUARANTEED HOME IMPACTS, IMPRESSIONS.

ghosted view. Picture providing x-ray view of subject. *See* EXPLODED DRAWING.

gift coupon. SALES PROMOTION method of encouraging regular purchases/habit buying by giving coupons with products which can be redeemed for gifts in a catalogue. Used by cigarette companies.

glams. Acronym for the PSYCHOGRAPHIC type 'greying leisured affluent middle-aged'. Subdivisions: glams 1... upmarket; glams 2...downmarket and usually older. Glams 2 were originally termed oldies, but this was discarded as indiscreet. *See* JOLLIES.

glass painting. Creation of illusionary backgrounds (rather like a back projection shot in films) for TV commercials. The view is painted on a glass sheet and the action is shot through the glass.

global advertising. Possible when a product is universally acceptable, e.g. Coca Cola, Kodak film, but impractical when products have to be adapted or re-named to suit foreign markets. Advertisers have to be careful not to assume that a product that is popular in the home market will be accepted similarly overseas. Guinness, for example, have different brews, labels, slogans to suit foreign markets.

glossy. Misleading term sometimes applied to magazines, but true only of minority of up-market titles. In OFFSET-LITHO printing, glossy inks.

glueing. DIRECT MAIL shots can be given novel effects by applying different kinds of glue (remoistenable, self-adhesive, thermo-reactive) to various parts of the same sheet of paper.

glyphic. Chiselled style of typeface.

gobbet. Brief item of advertisement copy, isolated by white space.

gondola. Circular self-service display stand with 5–7 shelves.

gothic. Black-letter typeface similar to handwriting.

graduated tints. Treatment resembling air-brush effect which, with digital typesetting, can be applied to either individual characters, or to a background.

grain. Folded print should flow with grain in direction of fibres in machine-made paper so that the paper is tougher across the grain and easier to fold.

Grant projector. Studio device for enlarging or reducing layouts and artwork by viewing through screen.

graphic characters. Line, shape and other visual effects produced by computer.

Graphic Paintbox. Quantel's method of producing visual effects. Manipulates photographic images, produces four-colour film via scanner and provides high-resolution transparencies in any format for scanning or for hard-copy proofs.

graphic work. According to the COPYRIGHT, DESIGNS AND PATENTS ACT 1988, graphic work includes (a) any painting, drawing, diagram, map, chart or plan, and (b) any engraving, etching, lithograph, woodcut or similar work. *See* PHOTOGRAPH.

graphics. Pictures as distinct from lettering or typography.

grey literature. Published material which is not classed as 'published serials' and not usually held in libraries or catalogued, which has no international standard serial number (ISSN), international standard book number (ISBN) or American CODEN number. Probably originated in Germany in the 1950s (graue literatur). First used in English language in December 1978 at the British Library Conference on the subject, York. Includes house journals, news releases, brochures, advertisements.

grey panthers. *See* JOLLIES.

gridsheet. Grid of a page or type area printed on layout sheet. May be on semi-transparent paper on which designer can trace lettering. It is also used by printer or publisher for paste-up. Grid lines in pale blue which will not reproduce.

grips. Front edge of paper held by grippers on printing machine, not usually printed but trimmed, or printed and trimmed to provide bled-off effect.

gross margin method. Way of fixing advertising appropriation. Percentage of balance after deducting production and distribution costs from income. Fails to be effective method because it does not accept advertising as a distribution cost.

gross OTS. Calculation of coverage of an advertising campaign by measuring OPPORTUNITIES TO SEE for each advertisement. Can apply to press, TV, outdoor advertising.

gross rating points. radio IMPACTS expressed as a percentage of the population being measured. One rating point equals one per cent of the population. The population measured can be all people or any demographic group.

gross revenue. Income from TV advertising if all commercials transmitted were costed at maximum rate less special discounts.

groundprint. Satellite FOOTPRINT.

group interviews. *See* DISCUSSION GROUP.

guaranteed circulation. Way of providing a yardstick when selling advertisement space or airtime in anticipation of audited net sale (ABC) or audience figure (BARB). Often used when launching new publication, with rebate if estimated figures not realised.

guaranteed home impacts, impressions, home ratings. Basis of selling TV airtime depending on number of homes in which the commercial is likely to be seen.

guiding question. In FOCUSSED and group INTERVIEWS or DISCUSSION GROUPS, a question which enables the interviewer to keep control.

guilloche. Fanciful veined design as used on security documents but which can be applied to make coupons and vouchers look realistic.

guppies. Special interest groups and hobbyists.

gutter. Space or margin between a pair of pages, allowing for fold, or white space between unruled columns of text.

gutter crossing. Headline run across centre margins of facing pages as in a double-page spread.

H

h & j. Hyphenation and justification. *See* HYPHENLESS JUSTIFICA-TION.

hairline. Delicate stroke in a typeface.

halftone. A continuous tonal effect in an illustration such as a photograph or wash drawing, reproduced by imposing a dot screen. Artwork photographed through lined glass, or a screen laid on pictures according to printing process. The latter method is used for litho printing which generally uses finer screens than for letterpress printing. The advantage of this can be seen in modern newspapers in which picture reproduction has greatly improved.

halftone screen ratings. Metric in brackets: 50(20), 55(22), 60(24), 65(26), 75(30), 80(32), 85(34), 100(40), 120(48), 133(54), 150(60), 175(70), 200(80). Letterpress newspapers mostly 65, offset-litho newspapers mostly 100.

hall test. Used for pre-testing products. Passers by are invited to answer questions in a hallway or other public place where the product is displayed or sampled. Also used for recall tests and other surveys.

halo effect. 1. In marketing research, bias caused by popularity or prior knowledge of the subject or product surveyed. 2. In advertising, reflected glory which one product gains from another made by the same manufacturer, or by the CORPORATE IMAGE. 3. In printing, ink build-up at edges of characters and halftone dots.

handling house. *See* FULFILMENT HOUSE.

hanging indent. Opening paragraph of text which is set to wider measure than the following text, perhaps to the width of two columns.

hard-bound. Case-bound as distinct from paperback, as in book binding.

hard copy. Print out of a Prestel frame. Any written, typed or printed out copy (e.g. computer print-out).

hard sell. Very persuasive advertising. Opposite to quieter soft sell.

harmony, law of. In design, harmonious arrangement of elements of a layout to make a pleasing whole.

Harry Animation/Editing System. Full animation system which can be added to the PAINTBOX computerised graphic system.

Harvest. Database marketing information service used by advertising agencies. Has sections headed Newsfile, Market Overviews, Advertising Factfile, Product News, Factfinder, Demographics and Consumer Research. A Lopex company based at MEAL, London.

head-end. In cable television, the station which provides onward transmission. Location of satellite earth receiving station or dish.

head margin. White space at the top of a page.

head-on position. In outdoor advertising, a poster site facing on-coming traffic.

headliner. Phototypesetting machine which produces lines of large display type.

heat-sealing. Way of sealing plastic bags or envelopes by partly melting the open edge.

heat-set. On some four-colour offset-litho machines, means of drying each colour by passsing print through heat box before printing next colour.

heavy. Quality newspaper with AB readership such as *The Times*, *The Independent*, *Financial Times*, or *The Observer*.

heavy ITV viewers. *See* WEIGHT OF VIEWING.

Heli-Blimp. Advertising balloon, completely customised with painted design, or fitted with interchangeable banners. The Balloon Stable, Bristol.

hertz. Frequency measurement for broadcasting. One thousand cycles per second = one kilohertz. *See* FREQUENCY.

hickey. Defect on printed sheet caused by a speck of dust or other imperfection.

high-density plastic. As used for envelopes for mailing magazines and catalogues. Thin, strong, light-weight plastic film. *See also* HEAT-SEALING.

high key. Pale grey tonal values in a photograph, wash drawing, or other picture with continuous tones.

High Street redemption schemes. SALES PROMOTION schemes involving redemption of cash vouchers at stores. May be money-off vouchers printed in press advertisements, on packs delivered door-to-door. Also, schemes which give cash vouchers redeemable at other stores.

highlights. Lightest tonal values in the halftone of a photograph or other continuous tone picture.

hire purchase terms. Under the Advertisements (Hire Purchase) Act 1967, an advertisement for goods offered on hire purchase or credit sale must state: full cash price; total amount if instalments are paid; length of time covered by each payment; number of instalments required before delivery of goods. Act also has regulations regarding deposit, no deposit and interest rates. Further requirements under Consumer Credit Act 1974 and Unfair Contract Terms Act 1977.

historical method. Way of deciding advertising appropriation by repeating a previous sum with adjustments to meet higher costs.

History of Advertising Trust. Devoted to the study of advertising and marketing history. Has created collection of historical material. London.

HKS colours. Similar to the internationally used Pantone Matching System colours. HKS colours are commonly used in German speaking countries.

hoarding. A poster site, usually at roadside, for pasting 4-sheet, 16-sheet, 48-sheet or 64-sheet posters. Called billboard in USA whereas in Britain this is a small poster display as seen outside a shop. *See* PANEL.

hold-over audience. Audience inherited from a previous TV/radio show and which provides a ready-made audience for next programme.

holiday junkies. PSYCHOGRAPHIC TYPE that enjoys and takes many holidays.

hologram. Three-dimensional picture as seen on some charge cards. *See* HOLOGRAPHY. Model made of image which is bathed in laser light to record master from which to produce copies. Holovision, London.

holography. Photographic process in which laser is used to make a three-dimensional picture by splitting the laser's beam into two. One beam then illuminates a photographic plate (reference beam), and the second beam is reflected off the subject back on to the plate (subject beam). Produces realistic 3D effect.

Home ITV Homes. ITV homes in defined ITV region which receive transmissions from the network servicing that region.

honorific. Title used to precede a person's name such as Mr, Mrs, Miss or Ms.

horizontal advertising. Group or co-operative advertising, usually by trade association, to promote the industry or product, e.g. insurance or bricks. No specific firm or brand is advertised.

horizontal journal. Journal aimed at a wide, unspecialised readership with common interest, e.g. a news magazine.

horizontal marketing. Extending the existing market, for instance, by selling accessories to original buyers. Opposite of vertical marketing.

horizontal trade journals. Journals read by people of similar status, e.g. company accountants, hotel managers or factory managers. Opposite of VERTICAL TRADE JOURNALS.

hot-air balloons. Aerial medium for advertising and PR purposes. Large and colourful, they attract attention as they travel overhead or feature at events, bearing large brand names and logos. *See* INFLATABLES.

hot-line list. Latest names added to a mailing list, and separated as such.

hot media. Non-participatory media such as press and radio. *See* COOL MEDIA, MCLUHAN, MARSHALL.

hot metal. Metal type as produced by Monotype and Linotype machines for LETTERPRESS printing. Mostly replaced by computerised PHOTOTYPESETTING. *See also* DIRECT INPUT.

house agency. Complete in-house agency found in some large companies which advertise regularly and at short notice and find it economic to handle the whole operation, as in some travel firms and stores. Usually able to obtain commission on media purchases.

house corrections. Proof corrections made by the printer before submitting proofs to client.

house list. MAILING LIST compiled in-house as distinct from external list bought or hired.

house style. Part of CORPORATE IDENTITY, standard printing style supported by style manual and relating to colour, typography, use of logo.

house-to-house distribution. DOOR-TO-DOOR DISTRIBUTION of sales and sales promotion material. Direct advertising. *See* MAIL DROP.

Household Delivery Service. Royal Mail HOUSE-TO-HOUSE DISTRIBUTION of unaddressed promotional material.

hyphenation. Programming of computerised typesetting to break words correctly at line ends.

hyphenless justification. Justification of lines of type without breaking words, which can produce gaps between words. This can look bad in narrow measures, columns, or ugly condensed settings.

I

IAMA. *See* INCORPORATED ADVERTISING MANAGEMENT ASSOCIATION.

IBA. *See* INDEPENDENT BROADCASTING AUTHORITY.

iconic medium. A medium such as film, video or television in which images have realism.

identification of author or director. *See* MORAL RIGHTS (under COPYRIGHT, DESIGNS AND PATENTS ACT 1988).

IDU. Indoor unit which decodes satellite signal for TV reception.

illicit recording. Under Section 197 of the COPYRIGHT, DESIGNS AND PATENTS ACT 1988, and for the purposes of a performer's rights, a recording of the whole or any substantial part of a performance of his is an illicit recording if it is made, otherwise than for private purposes, without his consent.

illuminated interior panels. Bus advertising positions on lower deck of double deckers, usually rented for minimum of 12 months.

illuminated posters. Rear illuminated posters or light boxes displayed in public places such as stores, shopping precincts, hotel lounges, Post Offices, airports, seaports, multi-storey car parks, buses. *See* ILLUMINATED INTERIOR PANELS, ROTASIGN.

illustration. Any pictorial representation, especially when reproduced in print.

ILR. *See* INDEPENDENT LOCAL RADIO.

image. The perceived image of an organisation based on knowledge and experience. In printing, printing areas of litho plate.

image master. Photographic original, or film master, for photosetting founts of type.

imitation art. Printing paper commonly used for printing magazines. Has china clay added to wood pulp. Calendered through hot and cold steel rollers to provide polished surface.

impact. The effect advertising has on readers, viewers or listeners. Awareness of advertisement, TV campaign can aim to achieve certain number of impacts per viewer.

Impact of Broadcast Advertising, The. 1987. In-depth study commissioned by Capital Radio. Objectives: measure the noticeability (impact) of advertising on radio and television; provide a commercials database to assess effect of commercial lengths, content, timing and scheduling on advertising impact; provide weightings for existing BARB and JICRAR ratings that reflect the impact rather than the presence. The study was conducted by means of 706 full stage interviews in the London area. A near-coincidental and recall technique, covering peak viewing and listening times for each medium, it was possible to measure opportunity to RECALL and POSITIVE RECALL RATING. With PRR the score can be used to evaluate broadcast campaigns as a weight for media planning and as a factor in determining a commercial's style and length.

impact testing. Advertisement research to measure impact as in RECALL SURVEYS.

impactive. An advertisement is said to be impactive when it achieves desired response.

impacts. Gross impressions, or the total number of exposures to a schedule of radio advertisements. Not a measure of the number of different people exposed to a commercial. *See* FREQUENCY.

imposition. In printing, arrangement of sequence of pages so that 8, 12 or 16 pages may be printed together in order to cut and fold correctly for assembly or binding.

imposition table. Table on which artwork and filmed typesettings are laid out or imposed for photographing in order to make plates for litho printing or sleeves for PHOTOGRAVURE printing.

impression. As in impression cylinder which presses inked plate against paper to produce an impression, that is a piece of print. In OFFSET LITHO plate cylinder prints on to blanket and impression cylinder holds paper against blanket cylinder to get off-set impression. Also, complete run of a piece of print called an impression, hence first impression (or edition) of a book.

imprint. Identity of publisher and/or printer stated on piece of print, useful so that printer can prove a legal claim for payment.

impulse buying. Unplanned purchase of goods which are specially displayed in stores using various POS devices and sales promotion schemes such as DUMP BINS, FLASH PACKS, and BANDED PACKS.

incentive schemes. mystery gift, ORDER BUILDING INCENTIVE, TWO-STEP GIFT LEADS as used in DIRECT RESPONSE marketing.

Incorporated Advertising Management Association. Professional society representing those responsible for advertising, publicity, sales promotion, marketing and public relations of commercial, public and other organisations.

Incorporated Society of British Advertisers. Trade association for protection and advancement of advertising interests of member firms. Advises on exhibitions, sponsorships, direct mail, media buying. London.

incredible concepts. Unusual ideas used in TV commercials, using strange figures, talking products, animation or computer graphics.

indent. To begin a paragraph with a space, as in BOOK STYLE used in books and newspapers. The first paragraph is usually set FULL-OUT or not indented. Indention makes print more readable than block paragraphs used in business letters. It encourages eye to read on.

Independent Broadcasting Authority. 1972. Replaced Independent Television Authority, 1955, to incorporate commercial radio. Public authority governing commercial radio and television in the UK. Awards station contracts. Provides transmitters. Operates Code of Advertising Standards and Practice, which goes further than BCAP, banning cigarette advertising, and ones dealing with politics, religion or public controversy. Very protective regarding child viewers. But *see* BROADCASTING IN THE 90s: COMPETITION, CHOICE AND QUALITY, White Paper published by Government November 8, 1988.

Independent Local Radio. Local commercial radio introduced by Sound Broadcasting Act, 1972. Latecomer to British advertising, commercials being broadcast by stations outside Britain such as Radio Luxembourg. In 1989, there are 44 ILR stations, using AM and FM frequencies, leasing transmitters from Independent Broadcasting Authority. But *see* RADIO AUTHORITY.

independent radio. British commercial radio. Term which has tended to replace original independent local radio (ILR).

Independent Television Association. Formerly Independent Television Companies Association. Represents TV programme companies as appointed by IBA. Vets TV and radio commercials with IBA before transmission, although IBA concentrates on sensitive areas such as advertising for alcohol, charities, share offers, condoms and sanitary protection.

Independent Television Authority. As announced in Government White Paper on broadcasting introduced November 7, 1988, the ITA replaces the Independent Broadcasting Authority and Cable Authority to control all commercial TV however delivered to viewers, but with no control over programme standards.

indirect printing. Process such as OFFSET-LITHO in which printing plate does not touch paper.

industrial advertising. Advertising conducted by suppliers to industry or trades and not to the consumer public. Uses trade and technical press, direct mail, trade exhibitions.

inflatables. Balloons in every kind of shape including packages or trade figures, tethered at vantage points and visible over considerable distance.

in-flight magazines. Magazines published by airlines and distributed to passengers by means of a pocket on the back of the seat. Copies also supplied by post.

in-flight movie commercials. Shown to airline passengers with in-flight movies.

informant, interviewee, respondent. Person asked questions or to test a product during a survey.

information providers. Those who supply information stored on PRESTEL computer for calling up by viewers equipped to receive prestel, page numbers given in Prestel Main Index.

inherited audience. Carry-over audience from a previous TV or radio programme. The HOLD-OVER AUDIENCE.

in-home placement. In product pre-testing, inviting people to test a product in daily use and complete questionnaire on it.

ink-jet printing. Computer-controlled printing process in which there is no direct contact between printing head and material being printed. Small droplets of electronically charged ink, as instructed by magnetic tape, are directed from printing head to surface. Used on fast reel-fed printing machines, cheaper than LASER PRINTING, ideal for addressing. Often used for DIRECT MAIL.

in-pack. Item, such as free gift, inserted in pack while the product is being packed. A Waddington inserter can place coupons, gifts and other items in packs on packaging line.

in-pro. In proportion. Instruction for enlarging or reducing photographs for reproduction.

insert, inset. Placing of loose advertisements in publications. Great increase in use of inserts, and publishers with modern plants have machines for placing inserts. Saves postage if material otherwise direct mailed, but inserts liable to be tipped out and discarded by readers. More successful if insert is of similar size to page of journal.

insert envelopes. Envelopes inserted inside DIRECT MAIL shots, perhaps acting as teasers, containing a special offer, a prize offer, or a gimmick. May be plain or printed. May convert a static advertisement into something more active, or may provoke overkill.

Insignia. Conducted by Marplan for CAA. 24-hour recall of 20–34 year old cinemagoers which has shown that one exposure on cinema can have a four times greater impact and memorability than one exposure on TV. An advantage of cinema advertising over TV advertising is that there are no NATURAL BREAKS, screen ads appearing between films.

instant on-pack coupons. Ones which can be cut from packet such as cash voucher against future purchase and redeemable at check-out.

Institute of Practitioners in Advertising. 1917. Professional body representing service advertising agencies. Holds annual Advertising Effectiveness Awards. London.

Institute of Sales Promotion. Professional body representing sales promotion firms. Holds annual awards. Has Diploma examination. Recommends rules for prize competitions. London.

Institute of Sales Promotion Consultancies, The. 1988. Breakaway from INSTITUTE OF SALES PROMOTION to provide trade association of firms supplying sales promotion consultancy services. Retains link with ISP, and works closely with CAM which now includes sales promotion exam papers at both levels.

institutional advertising. Corporate image or prestige advertising, usually found in business press. Kind of PR advertising, used to establish reputation. *See* ADVOCACY/ISSUE ADVERTISING.

in-store interview. Form of marketing research when respondents are interviewed while shopping.

in-store promotion. SALES PROMOTION technique involving sampling or demonstration inside store.

intaglio. Printing process in which an image is recessed below surface of plate as with PHOTOGRAVURE and copper engraving.

integration. Concept of unifying the media, especially the addition of DIRECT MAIL to existing advertising and SALES PROMOTION campaigns. Critics consider such a single strategic plan and budget as impractical, and that DIRECT RESPONSE marketing should be regarded as a separate new marketing force.

intellectual property. Company, product and service names that are registered and legally protected.

intellectual property rights. These are distinguished into two kinds: all written matter protected by copyright, and skill and expertise which is partly confidential is legally protected. There are intellectual property rights (IPRs). The COPYRIGHT, DESIGNS AND PATENTS ACT 1988 provided new legal protection for designs and introduced new criminal offences to protect trademarks. IPRs consist of the following assets: confidentiality, copyright, trademark or service mark, patent, registered design, or unregistered design. *See* MORAL RIGHTS.

Intelsat VA F11. Multi-channel satellite including CNN, Children's Channel, Premiere.

INTELSTAT. International telecommunications satellite organisation.

interactive cable TV. As introduced by W. H. Smith Cable, system whereby the viewer can switch on TV and ask it to show them what they wish to watch. Useful for DIRECT RESPONSE marketing.

interfacing. Getting one computer to talk to another as when a text generated on one computer cannot automatically be read by another. The author or client's floppy disk will not drive the printer's laser typesetting computer until it has been interfaced through the printer's multi-disk reader. This is because different disks have different directions, may slow down or speed up as they spin, or be single-sided, double-sided, hard-sectored or soft-sectored, and they may store data in their own peculiar ways. Also, the author may use a particular software package, many of which have non-standard control codes.

interleaves. Sheets of paper inserted between printed sheets to prevent set-off from wet ink. Also, placing of paper of a different kind between text pages, especially to print pictures on a better class of paper.

International Code of Advertising Practice. Originally published by the International Chamber of Commerce in 1937. Model for BRITISH CODE OF ADVERTISING PRACTICE. Used by more than 250 advertising associations in some 35 countries. One of series of International Codes of Marketing Practice which also includes ICC Code of Sales Promotion Practice. Paris.

International Journal of Advertising. Quarterly review published for the Advertising Association by Holt, Rinehart and Winston Ltd, Eastbourne.

International Reply Service. DIRECT MAIL reply service offered by bulk international mailing services TNT MAILFAST. Enhances possibilities of cross-border trading. Mailfast also offer dedicated Post Office Box services in 32 countries and advise on business reply paid specifications in foreign countries.

interval sample. *See* RANDOM SAMPLE.

interviewer. Person who conducts research surveys. Should be capable of restraining bias. Much field work is conducted by part-time interviewers, trained for the task. They should carry a card identifying the organisation responsible for the survey, although not its sponsors. These cards are supplied by the MARKET RESEARCH SOCIETY and ASSOCIATION OF MARKET SURVEY ORGANIZATIONS.

interviewer-supported panel. Research panel whose members are visited regularly to check purchases and packages are retained for inspection by interviewer. Rather like DUSTBIN CHECK. For example *see* TELEVISION CONSUMER AUDIT.

in-theatre research. Used to pre-test TV commercials and also posters. The audience is assembled in a theatre or hall and shown the advertisements. They may be asked which product they would prefer as a gift, or would buy, both before and after being shown as TV commercial.

IPA. *See* INSTITUTE OF PRACTITIONERS IN ADVERTISING.

IPA Direct Marketing Group. Formed 1989. Aims to raise recognition and standing of direct marketing in the advertising industry. Code of Practice as professional standard for the industry. Seeks to cross-fertilise training between general advertising and direct marketing via IPA and Direct Marketing Centre courses. London.

IPR. *See* INTELLECTUAL PROPERTY RIGHTS.

IR. *See* INDEPENDENT RADIO.

IRS. *See* INTERNATIONAL REPLY SERVICE.

ISBA. *See* INCORPORATED SOCIETY OF BRITISH ADVERTISERS.

island sites. Press advertisement surrounded on at least three sides by editorial. Exhibition site with aisles on all sides. SOLUS site.

ISP. *See* INSTITUTE OF SALES PROMOTION.

issue advertising. *See* ADVOCACY/ISSUE ADVERTISING.

ITA. *See* INDEPENDENT TELEVISION ASSOCIATION.

italic. Typeface which slopes to the right. Invented by Italian printer, Aldus Manutius, 15th century.

ITV areas. At present the 13 regions covered by the 15 commercial TV contractors, London having two, one weekday and one weekend. The areas are: London, East and West Midlands, North West, Yorkshire, North East, East of England, South and South-East, South-West, Ulster, Border, Central Scotland, North Scotland, and Wales and the West. An area is served by a transmitter or group of transmitters. Liable to change when ITA replaces IBA, ITV becomes CHANNEL THREE, and stations are auctioned instead of being awarded franchises.

ITV boundary line. Agreed marking of the limit of effective reception for a transmitter or transmitters in an ITV area.

ITVA. *See* INDEPENDENT TELEVISION ASSOCIATION. Previously ITCA.

J

jack. Plug for connecting a television set to the telephone to receive PRESTEL viewdata.

JICCAR. *See* JOINT INDUSTRY COMMITTEE FOR CABLE AUDIENCE RESEARCH.

JICMARS. *See* JOINT INDUSTRY COMMITTEE OF MEDICAL ADVERTISERS FOR READERSHIP SURVEYS.

JICNARS. *See* JOINT INDUSTRY COMMITTEE FOR NATIONAL READERSHIP SURVEYS.

JICPAR. *See* JOINT INDUSTRY COMMITTEE FOR POSTER AUDIENCE RESEARCH.

JICRAR. *See* JOINT INDUSTRY COMMITTEE FOR RADIO AUDIENCE RESEARCH.

jiffy-bags. Lightweight protective envelopes, padded or with bubble-cushioning. Jiffy Packaging Co. Winsford.

jingles. Tunes with slogans or DOGGEREL used in TV and radio commercials, and often repeated in other advertising.

job sheet. Systematic record of work in progress, stating job number, and client code, on which agent or other supplier such as printer logs expenditures as ordered, progressed and supplied. Essential to efficient charging out of accounts to clients.

Joint Industry Committee for Cable Audience Research. Publishes quarterly establishment data showing the number of homes passed by and connected by cable. Also publishes reports on viewing habits in cable homes.

Joint Industry Committee of Medical Advertisers for Readership Surveys. Serves subscriber publishers, pharmaceutical companies and pharmaceutical advertising agencies by supplying data on readership of medical publications by

UK general practitioners, in order to assist media planning. London.

Joint Industry Committee for National Readership Surveys. Tripartite body representing advertisers, agencies and publishers through their trade bodies, responsible for the National Readership Survey. A continuous survey comprising 30,000 annual interviews is conducted to estimate READERSHIP and readership profiles of newspapers and magazines. Classifies respondents by SOCIAL GRADES A, B, C^1, C^2, D, E, based on employment rather than income. London.

Joint Industry Committee for Poster Audience Research. Has made a number of studies of the audience for poster advertising. Now associated with OSCAR.

Joint Industry Committee for Radio Audience Research. Tripartite body representing advertisers, agencies, and ILR contractors and conducts research into radio audiences. London.

jollies. Jet-setting oldies with lots of loot, people aged 49–59 with paid-off mortgage, married children, husband retired early, free of financial pressures. They form nearly 9% of population. Disposable income about £108b. Market for luxury goods including travel (e.g. Saga). Alternative names: GREY PANTHERS, WOOPIES, GLAMS.

Journal of Advertising History. Articles on great campaigns, outstanding characters and social consequences of advertising. Published twice yearly for HISTORY OF ADVERTISING TRUST by MCB University Press, Bradford. First published in 1977.

jumbo pack. SALES PROMOTION device, a number of associated brands such as individual packs of breakfast cereals or bars of chocolate are packed together. Often used at Christmas. Also, very large economy packs, jars and bottles for detergents or drinks.

junior unit. In press advertising, a standard page size advertisement that can be enlarged or reduced to fit different journals, or can be reproduced at the same size with or without next matter. If based on smallest size, the advertisement will not suffer from reduction making small type difficult to read.

junk cards. Plastic cards resembling credit cards but having no credit value, used for promotional purposes. May offer short-term privilege.

junk mail. Unsolicited but especially badly targeted, duplicated, wrongly addressed and generally careless DIRECT MAIL. Whether or not it is junk mail will depend on the response of the recipient. But sometimes applied to all direct mail as 'advertising which masquerades as personal post' (Miles Kington).

justification. Spacing out type matter to fill lines of equal length. More legible than if there is a free right hand edge.

juxtaposition. Unfortunate placing of rival advertisements next to one another.

K

K & N absorbency. Way of testing ink absorbency of various papers.

kaolin. Fine clay used in making papers such as IMITATION ART.

keeper gift. Gift made to encourage a request for information about an advertised product or service, or for a trial or sample. The enquirer is allowed to keep the gift, whether or not sale results.

kenaf. Tropical plant which offers cheap alternative to wood for making paper.

kern. In a typographical character, extension beyond body such as tail of a 'y'.

kettle stitches. Stitches which sew together SIGNATURES of a book.

key. Device which enables advertiser to identify source of enquiry as when a coupon has an unobtrusive key printed in the corner (e.g. DM5 meaning fifth insertion in the *Daily Mail*). Keys can be included in the address. A different person's name can be used in each journal, or there can be a variation in the address such as 11a, 11b, 11c. By means of keys it is possible to calculate the cost-per-reply by dividing the cost of the space by the number of enquiries. Similarly, cost per conversion to sales can be calculated.

key forme. In colour printing, the plate which is used first.

key region radio. Those used by MEAL for continuous complementary monitor of brand expenditure on radio. Account for 70% of commercial radio (ILR) revenue. Ten major contractors placed in six primary marketing areas: London (Capital, LBC); Midlands (BRMB, Trent); Lancashire (Piccadilly, City); Yorkshire (Aire, Hallam); North East (Metro); Scotland (Clyde)

key size. Unit of type measurement in phototypesetting.

keyline, key drawing. Outline used for positioning artwork in a piece of print.

keystroke. Depression of a keyboard key as with direct input in a computerised newsroom, or with computerised phototype-setting.

kicker. Short line of copy set in smaller type above a headline.

kids oral satisfaction market. Products bought by children with pocket money to burn, e.g. crisps, soft drinks, sweets, and pressing parents to buy lolly freezers and Italian ice cream makers.

kill. Delete unwanted typesettings.

kiss impression. Very light printing impression.

Klischograph hard-dot gravure. Advance on traditional recessed PHOTOGRAVURE where the plate has surface areas of various sizes to give depths of tone instead of cells of various depths.

knock down. Dismantling of exhibition stand at close of show.

knocking copy. *See* ASHCANNING, DENIGRATION.

kodatrace. Clean film overlay placed on artwork, with extra instructions to printer.

KOSM. *See* KIDS ORAL SATISFACTION MARKET.

KpH. Body height of a typeface. *See also* AH and PH.

Kroy lettering centre. Desk-top micro-computer with 'qwerty' keyboard, capable of producing thousands of different character sizes and style variations. Kroy (Europe) Ltd, London.

L

L-side. Bus side advertisement space with horizontal bus side position on double decker plus vertical space at rear.

laid paper. Paper with parallel watermark lines.

Lamb, Charles. Author and poet who was one of the first copy-writers, writing Government lottery advertisements in 1800. He helped James White to set up Britain's first advertising agency.

laminate. To give print a glossy, protective finish by sticking transparent plastic film to the surface. Used for covers of brochures/books, record sleeves, picture postcards. Similarly, artwork and proofs may be so protected.

landscape. Horizontal page or picture, wider than it is deep.

language inflation. Repeated use of words such as new, good, free, now, and special, which may seem banal and yet can be effective clichés of copywriting. *See* BUZZ WORDS.

language noise. Expressions which cause misunderstanding because they are capable of having double meanings. It may even be an offensive meaning in another language or culture. Nigger brown was once a common colour, but because of racial implications it is rarely used today. Baby's Bottom was a brand of tobacco, which had to be withdrawn. Swarfega suggests metal waste, but swarf means clean in Derbyshire.

laser. Acronym meaning light amplification by stimulated emission of radiation. A narrow beam of light used to create images, as in Linotronic computerised typesetting machine.

laser printing. Much used in DIRECT MAIL printing for typographical and colour effects and PERSONALISATION within sales letters. Operates by means of a photo-conductive material which holds the image of individually produced characters by low-power laser-beam scanning material. Image coated with toner which is then transferred to the printing surface by a heated roller. Computer software is applied and each character is individually produced at up to 10,000 per hour.

latex silver scratch off. DIRECT MAIL or SALES PROMOTION device, a protective silver latex coating being scratched off to reveal, for instance, lucky number.

lay down. Impose a print job. *See* IMPOSITION TABLE.

layout. Plan or design of an advertisement or piece of print, exactly set out as distinct from a VISUAL, with measured areas for type and illustrations and display lines drawn, together with typographical instructions, for the printer to follow. May be finished up to show client what the job will look like, or to serve as guide to making up camera-ready artwork.

lead generation. Advertising which produces sales leads, especially by means of coupons.

leaders. Dots and lines that direct the reader's eye in lists, e.g. completing the line between words and prices.

leaf. A single sheet comprising two pages, back and front.

ledger. Strong, good quality smooth writing paper used for documents, accounts books.

legend. *See* CAPTION.

legged efforts. Bonus sales which occur when advertising continues to produce results after a campaign has ended and in excess of the target. Some couponed advertisements in magazines may go on producing replies for months afterwards.

Letrachrome. Letraset colour imaging system.

Letrajet. Letraset device which converts a Pantone marker into an airbrush.

Letraset. Make of DRY TRANSFER LETTERING consisting of sheets of ready-printed characters which can be transferred to paper by rubbing.

letterbox marketing. Direct advertising using the distribution services of free newspapers for home deliveries of mail shots or doorstoppers. In UK 18.5m homes can be reached in three days every week. Household targeting (e.g. ACORN), can be applied to reach socio-economic groupings in specific neighbourhoods.

letterpress. Relief printing process. All printing areas are raised to take ink and transfer this to paper. Similar to a date stamp. There are three kinds of machines; platen, flat-bed and rotary. Largely superseded by OFFSET-LITHO as in newspaper industry.

letterspacing. Increasing emphasis by spacing out characters, as in display lines.

LF. *See* LINE FEED.

LF/CH. *See* LINE FEED FACTOR.

library music. Recorded music on disc or tape held by music libraries which may be hired for a fee to use as background music in TV commercials, films or videos.

library shot. Either specially taken film (e.g. of famous locations, airliners taking off, in flight and landing), or scenes from existing films, which can be inserted in new productions such as TV commercials. Supplied by film libraries and archivists. Companies (such as airlines, tourist organisations) may shoot pictures for such purposes by other users.

licensing. On payment of fees a provision of rights to use proprietary names, figures, characters for promotional purposes, e.g. Disney cartoon characters, Muppets. *See* CHARACTER MERCHANDISING.

lifestyle survey. Facts of Living survey conducted by database marketing firm ICD Direct. Questions inserted by sponsors on lengthy survey are distributed to 15m respondents with an offer of shopping vouchers. For example, 1m mailed to ICD in-house list, 5.5m inserted in *Radio Times*, *You Magazine*, *Observer Magazine*, 8.5m delivered door-to-door.

ligature. Letters joined together on one type body.

light reader. Revealed in a *TV Times* 'How People Read' survey, conducted by BMP Solutions in Media, that more than one third of adults spend less than 4.5 hours a week on leisure reading. 25.4% classified as light readers. Those who read for less than two hours amounted to 11.7%. Spread over all social grades. Not necessarily LIGHT VIEWERS, more likely, HEAVY VIEWERS.

light viewer. Those of higher social grades or whose activities reduce their possible viewing time, who watch less television than majority of viewers. About 30% of viewers watching only 9% of TV transmitted. *See* WEIGHT OF VIEWING.

lightboxes. *See* ILLUMINATED POSTERS.

line gauge. Type rule with different point sizes, used for COPY-FITTING and measuring type.

line mechanical. Paste-up of line copy ready to photograph for making litho plate.

linespacing. Spacing between lines of photoset type.

line-by-line. Selection of outdoor advertising positions site-by-site from a poster contractor's list. Or cinema advertising by precise geographical targeting. Campaigns can be targeted at certain towns or for one or any number of weeks.

line drawing. An open drawing with no shaded areas, made up of lines, dots and solids.

linefeed. In phototypesetting, means of inserting space between lines of type.

Line Feed. In digital typesetting, equivalent of set solid, i.e. without leading or white space between lines of type. Baseline to baseline distance in mm.

Line Feed Factor. In digital typesetting, a value (e.g. 1.6) used to multiply capital height of a typeface, which is then divided by 18 to produce one unit for spacing purposes.

lineale. Sans-serif type face.

linear graduated screens. Use of vertical and horizontal graduated halftone screens, for both black and white and colour printing, to give a shaded or almost airbrush effect, by means of digital typesetting. *See* PROGRESSIVE GRADUATED SCREENS, SCANTEX 2000.

list broker. Specialist in supplying MAILING LISTS, or print-outs from them, to DIRECT MAIL users. May offer services such as research, selection, recommendation and eventual evaluation.

list cleaning. Process of removing out-of-date, duplicated or otherwise unwanted names and addresses from a MAILING LIST.

list exchange. Barter arrangement between companies for the use of each other's mailing lists.

list maintenance. Manual or computer system for regular update of MAILING LISTS, such as deletions of invalid addresses and addition of new ones.

list malfunction. Weakness of a MAILING LIST because it contains duplications and errors which are difficult to detect and amend because of variations in data.

list manager. Employee of the owner of a MAILING LIST who maintains it, is responsible for its use, and may market it.

list rental. Supply of a MAILING LIST on a one-time-only retail basis. Lists of members, donors, customers rented to those who wish to make DIRECT MARKETING offers to the same people. Can be profitable practice for owners of useful lists.

list sample. Selection of names taken from a mailing for a test mailing to measure responsiveness of the list.

list selection. Characteristics used to select certain groups of names and addresses, as with a DATABASE when filters can be included in the software so that particular names can be called up and printed.

listening. In commercial radio research, listening is recorded in terms of 15 min. segments and is defined as 'any listening' within a particular segment. Between midnight and 0600 hours listening is recorded in 30 minute segments. *See* TOTAL HOURS.

listings. Term for radio and television programme details. In Britain, publication of programmes is restricted to the day of broadcast in newspapers, with highlighted information in other journals. *Radio Times* and *TV Times* monopolise listings for the week ahead. With the sale of *TV Times* and other changes under new broadcasting legislation, the listings monopoly is unlikely to survive.

literal. Printer's typesetting error, which printer is responsible for making correction without charge. Not an author's correction.

literary work. According to the COPYRIGHT, DESIGNS AND PATENTS ACT 1988, literary work means any work, other than a dramatic or musical work, which is written, spoken or sung, inclusive of a table or compilation, and a computer program.

lithography. Planographic printing process based on principle that water and grease will not mix. Invented by John Aloysius Senefelder in Munich, 1796. With the original system, image was drawn in reverse on porous stone. For posters artists had to draw design in reverse for each colour to be printed. With introduction of photography, metal plates replaced stone. *See* DIRECT LITHO, WEB-OFFSET-LITHO.

litter-bin advertising. Supply of street litter bins by contractor, on which advertising space is sold, or advertiser sponsors a litter bin bearing his name.

livery. Form of CORPORATE IDENTITY, vehicles, ships, aircraft, railway wagons, distinguished by company's HOUSE STYLE, name display, LOGOTYPE or other designs. Historical origins: emblems on soldiers' shields or sails of ships, colours of stage coaches, leading up to ship's funnels and currently airliners.

loaded question. To be avoided in a marketing research questionnaire because it implies an expected answer and is biased.

logotype. Often abbreviated to logo. Part of corporate identity scheme, a visual presentation of a company name. Often in a special shape like a badge, or using handwriting as with Ford, Cadbury, Coca-Cola logos, or special lettering. Can be registered as trade mark but may be additional to trade mark. *See* SYMBOL.

lombard. Acronym for PSYCHOGRAPHIC TYPE, lots of money but a real dickhead.

London Chamber of Commerce and Industry. 1851. Has Examinations Board and offers Third Level Certificate and Group Diplomas in Advertising, Marketing, Public Relations and Selling and Sales Management. Oldest and largest independent British examining body in business studies subjects. Has centres world-wide, and handles half-million exam scripts annually for all its subjects. ALCC qualification for Diploma holders. Sidcup, Kent.

loss leader. Product offered by retailer at very low price to attract trade.

lower case. Small letters in typesetting. Originates from hand setting when small letters kept in lower case or drawer of type-cabinet containing individual type characters. *See* UPPER CASE.

Lupin database. Large survey of shopping patterns. Defines shopping catchment areas, having asked consumers at home where they shop. Telephone interviewing is also used. Also provides shopper flow data between home locations and shopping centres. Used by Pinpoint Analysis Ltd.

M

machine coated. Paper which is coated or given a special surface on the papermaking machine.

machine proof. Proof which is checked at the printers, as often as necessary with colour printing to avoid holding up the machine.

macro-media. Mass circulation or mass audience media such as press, radio, TV, cinema.

magalogue. Free magazine, usually distributed to AB readers, and containing expensive items mostly bought by charge-card holders.

magazine. Large blocks of specialised information offered by PRESTEL.

magazine-card. Promotional vehicle consisting of a card formed by a perforation on a magazine cover, the card being protected and re-inforced by a resistant PVC film. Can be used for claiming a benefit such as a discount on a purchase. Morley-Cox Ltd, Bromley, Kent.

magenta. Shade of beetroot red used in four-colour printing.

mail drop. Advertisement delivered door-to-door.

mail-in. Form of SALES PROMOTION in which the applicant sends in a coupon from a press advertisement or token from a pack for a free offer. There may be a small charge for postage and payment, but it is not a premium offer requiring payment for a special price offer. Alternatively, a cash refund or cash voucher may be offered.

mail order. Trading by post. Now mostly called DIRECT RESPONSE marketing. Not to be confused with DIRECT MAIL which is an advertising medium. Mail order is conducted by direct mail, catalogues, OFF-THE-PAGE press advertisements, TV, etc. The big growth area has been financial services.

Mail Order Protection Scheme. Reader protection scheme run by NEWSPAPER PUBLISHERS' ASSOCIATION and PERIODICAL PUBLISHERS' ASSOCIATION regarding displaying advertisements in British newspapers and magazines. MOPS advertisements appear in the press. Advertisers are vetted and have to pay into a central fund which is used to compensate a reader who loses money because a trader goes out of business. Excludes classified ads, goods on approval and certain other categories.

mail order publisher. Publisher who sells books, magazines, gramophone records, cassettes, compact discs, videos and other publications by post, such as book and record clubs or a subscription publisher.

Mail Order Transactions (Information Order) 1976. Order, made under the Fair Trading Act, requires statement of the trader's name and address in mail order advertisements.

mailing list. List of prospects used in DIRECT RESPONSE marketing. Important that this list is up-to-date, and is frequently purged of dead addresses or de-duplicated, especially when several lists which can include repeat addresses are being used.

Mailing Preference Service. Run by six trade associations, with Post Office support, enables members of the public to have their names either removed from or added to mailing lists. Requests are sent regularly to member firms holding mailing lists or databases. London. 1983.

mailing response analysis. Use of regression techniques to measure neighbourhood characteristics which seem to deliver the best mailing response. Then possible to score postcodes in a prospect-scoring model which seeks to maximise response from a later mailing. French Coref system used by Pinpoint Analysis Ltd.

Mailsort. Royal Mail service aimed at national standardisation of terms: common entry qualification for each Mailsort service; improved presortation methods. Replaces former Rebate system and places better responsibility on DIRECT MAIL users to presort mail, and offers higher discounts for presorted mail. Previously, pre-sortation systems were based on Town and Country sorts but, as the WWAV GROUP GUIDE TO MAILSORT points out, the Post Office delivery office for any given area is not necessarily geographically located in that area; conversely there may be three or four (or more) delivery offices in a large town or city. Under the Mailsort Flexiplan some 1,600 sortations are possible so that mail can be directed quickly to the office of delivery.

Mailwatch. 1989. Set up by DIRECT MAIL SERVICES STANDARDS BOARD to supervise direct mail practice on similar lines to the ADVERTISING STANDARDS AUTHORITY, and to handle public complaints.

Main Index. Catalogue of services available on PRESTEL.

makegood. Re-run of press advertisement or TV/radio commercial following a dispute or failure to insert or transmit as scheduled.

malredemption. Malpractice of abusing coupon offers by theft from printers or stores, or other criminal misuse of premium offers. Term loosely used for MISREDEMPTION.

managing mums. Psychographic group consisting of guilt-ridden women dedicated to keeping husband and children happy. *See* PSYCHOGRAPHIC TYPES.

mapping. Graphic geodemographic reports to show customer density and penetration, target markets and areas of business density. Part of Insight service from Credit and Data Marketing Services Ltd, Liverpool. *See* SUPER PROFILES.

margins. In printing, back, head, fore-edge and tail, four to a page and best proportioned 1, 1½, 2 and 2½ respectively.

markas. Acronym for psychographic type middle-aged re-nester, kids away. *See* PSYCHOGRAPHIC TYPES.

marked proof. Proof bearing printer's corrections before it is submitted to the client.

market research. Study of the market, using various research techniques. Not to be confused with marketing research which includes all kinds of research relevant to marketing, such as advertisement and media research.

Market Research Society. Professional body for those using survey techniques for market, social and economic research. Has code of practice. London.

market segment. A section or sub-group of the total market as with special blends of coffee, or different sizes of cars. Advertisements need to be written, designed and placed according to the market segment they aim to reach. May be special interest groups or particular social grades. NICHE MARKETING.

market segmentation study. Research to define target groups for products. Pioneered in UK by Taylor, Nelson Research.

marketing. Management process responsible for identifying, anticipating and satisfying customer requirements profitably (CIM). Producing and selling at a profit what people want rather than simply trying to sell what has been made with no attempt to find out first whether it is likely to satisfy the market.

Marketing. News, features on marketing, sales promotion. London. 1964 (as weekly 1980).

marketing communications. Every element of the MARKETING MIX or strategy which involves communications with sales force, distributor and users/consumers. Not limited to promotional communications such as selling, advertising and sales promotion. Also includes public relations at all levels, and forms of communication such as branding, labelling, packaging, pricing and marketing research.

marketing mix. The marketing strategy consisting of all elements in the planning and operation of marketing such as branding, pricing, packaging, selling, distribution, advertising, sales promotion and marketing research. Public relations is an integral part of the mix since there are communications at most stages. *See also* MARKETING COMMUNICATIONS.

Marketing Pocket Book. Concise well-documented analysis of statistics including expenditure figures on advertising for each medium, and maps of standard regions (Nielsen regions, ITV areas, regional, daily and Sunday newspaper locations, independent radio stations and regions, and locations of superstores). The Advertising Association, annual, London.

marketing research. All kinds of scientific study applied to marketing, including pre-testing of advertisements, post-advertising research such as tracking studies, and media research such as that conducted by ABC, BARB, JICNARS, JICRAR, etc. This is broader than MARKET RESEARCH which is limited to studies of the market.

Marketing Week. News, features on advertising, media and marketing. London 1978. Weekly.

marque. Name or brand which distinguishes a product in a range of products such as different coffee blends or cars (e.g. Ford Escort, Sierra, Granada). This can also lead to a marque personality or image which attaches to a product, e.g. Porsche or Rolls-Royce.

married print. Film print or videotape combining picture and sound. *See* DOUBLE-HEAD.

masking. 1. Placing a protective layer over area(s) of a picture while retouching or AIRBRUSHING other parts. 2. Blocking out part of a picture to prevent it being reproduced, or to permit correction. 3. Way of adjusting colour values and tone in photomechanical reproduction.

mass market. Popular market for FMCGS, as distinct from made-to-order goods or luxury goods.

mass media. Media addressed to the MASS MARKET, e.g. popular press, radio, TV, outdoor, cinema.

master proof. GALLEY or PAGE PROOF, bearing printer's corrections, and submitted to author or client for corrections. New copy changes (author's corrections) liable to charge.

masthead. Distinctive title design of a newspaper or magazine. In readership surveys, cards bearing mastheads are used for recall purposes.

match code. An abbreviation of data taken from names and addresses on a MAILING LIST, so that editing or identification of the records is simplified.

matched panels. As used by Nielsen for HTV Stats-Scan service which exploits the split transmission facility of the HTV West and HTV Wales catchment areas. Panel matching variables include: size of household, social class, presence of children, age of housewife, household durables, e.g. freezer, weight of TV viewing, TV durables, e.g. multi-set ownership, VCR.

matt. Dull paper surface for finish.

matt calender. On papermaking machine, the cylinder which creates a smooth dull finish and bulk for blade-coated offset litho papers. Improves ink gloss.

MCAM. Designatory letters for CAM graduates who are members of the CAM Graduates Association. Otherwise, DipCAM.

McLuhan, Marshall. Canadian don who created concepts of HOT and COLD MEDIA. Famous for his expression 'the medium is the message'. Author of *The Mechanical Bride*, *The Gutenberg Galaxy*, and *Understanding Media*.

MEAD database. Offers full text service such as more than 17m articles, mostly American, but available in the UK. MEAD Data, London.

MEAL. *See* MEDIA EXPENDITURE ANALYSES LTD.

MEAL Quarterly Digest. *See* DIGEST OF BRANDS AND ADVERTISERS.

meanline. The X-HEIGHT of a typeface, that is of small letters without extensions, e.g. a, e, o. With some typefaces the x-height can be low, making type less legible in small point sizes. Such type is best used in large sizes for display purposes. This matter is to be considered when choosing typography for CORPORATE IDENTITY scheme.

Mecanorma. System of DRY TRANSFER LETTERING consisting of symbols, tones, screens to add to artwork. London.

mechanical. 1. Artwork for printing. 2. CAMERA-READY COPY. 3. Grade of printing paper made from woodpulp but containing lignin which discolours paper as when newsprint is exposed to light.

mechanical binding. Binding which opens flat. Useful for ring binders or spiral bound publications. Requires wide margin for punching to take binding.

mechanical data. As specified in media-owner's rate card or in BRAD, data setting out production details such as column lengths and widths, printing process, halftone screens and colour facilities.

mechanical pulp. Produced by grinding instead of through chemicals and used to make NEWSPRINT.

mechanical separations. Separate colour overlays in register with one another.

media. Means of communication such as press, radio, TV, film, video, exhibition, sales literature, direct mail, catalogues, telephone, posters, signs, newscasters, etc. Plural of medium.

media advertising. The traditional ABOVE-THE-LINE media, press, radio, TV, outdoor, cinema, and those on which advertising agencies relied for commission income, although many nowadays charge service fees.

media buyer. Executive in advertising agency (or large in-house advertising department) who negotiates purchase of space and airtime. Originally called space buyer. Large agencies have separate buyers of space and airtime, and also MEDIA PLANNERS.

media co-ordination. Way of buying media more competitively. One agency co-ordinates the media buying for different product accounts of one company which are handled creatively by other agencies.

media-demassification. As projected by TOFFLER, ALVIN in THE THIRD WAVE, the breakdown or fragmentation of the mass media to serve smaller readerships or audiences. Has happened in the newspaper field with newspapers having viable circulations of under half-a-million, and is being brought about by cable and satellite TV.

Media Expenditure Analyses Ltd. Better known as MEAL, provides reports and on-line services regarding brands and advertisers. These include: product group reports; Digest of Brands and Advertisers; On-line and PC Services (MEAL data on Donovan Data Systems, MEAL on your Micro); annual reports on top advertisers, top brands, ten year trends. Brands are attributed to 370 product groups, classified into 22 categories. Media coverage: TV, radio, popular dailies, quality dailies, popular Sundays, quality Sundays, weekend magazines, regional Sundays, regional mornings, regional evenings, general weeklies, general monthlies, women's weeklies, women's monthlies, and certain groups of special interest magazines. Inserts not recorded. Maintains largest data-base of advertising activity in UK. Each month more than 300,000 individual advertisements are attributed to more than 18,000 brands.

media explosion. Rapid development of new press, radio, TV, teletext and other media, aided by new publishing and broadcasting techniques which have occurred in recent years, including international media using satellite facilities.

media exposure analysis. Measuring and interpreting exposure of respondents to various media. Allowance necessary for those who may not read, see or hear certain media.

media independent. Advertising agency which plans and buys media but does no creative work. *See* ASSOCIATION OF MEDIA INDEPENDENTS.

media planner. Agency executive who plans media schedules for approval by client, using rate card details, circulation, readership and audience figures, to select the most economical and effective media to reach target market.

Media Register, The. Run by Advertising Research Services. Monitors advertising expenditure in competition with MEAL. Provides slides or prints of any roadside poster displayed, and supplies poster expenditure data.

media schedule. Plan of media bookings showing titles (or stations), dates, times, positions, costs.

Media Tel Viewdata Services. On-line media databases for advertising agencies and PR consultancies. In 1989, added a central source of sponsorship information with sponsorship availability index, giving details of sponsorship availability.

media tiredness. Failure of media to retain their pulling power due to excessive use. Necessary to determine the lowest number of insertions, spots or mailshots before law of decreasing returns applies.

Medicines Act, 1968. Stipulates that advertisements for medicines must conform to terms of licence issued by Medicines Commission in respect of each produce concerned. Also, Regulations issued by the Secretary of State for Social Services such as Medicines (Advertising of Medicinal Products) Regulations 1975, and Medicines (Advertising of Medicinal Products) (No.2) Regulations 1975.

megalists. Databases containing vast numbers of names and addresses for DIRECT MAIL purposes ranging from investors (e.g. share registers for privatisation) to customer, membership and donor list. Some databases are several million strong.

member-get-member incentives. SALES PROMOTION method by which members of charge card companies, book and record clubs, and associations receive gifts for enrolling or recommending new members or customers.

memory factor. Problem when conducting research surveys that respondents cannot always remember correctly. Even claim, for instance, to have seen an advertisement that has not appeared. Can be overcome by aided recall methods such as MASTHEADS of publication in READERSHIP SURVEYS or, better still, with diaries in which consumers record TV programmes watched or products bought.

merchandising. Former term for SALES PROMOTION which has been largely dropped because of its confusion with the retail term for selection and display of goods (merchandise).

merge. Combining of MAILING LISTS as occurs when names and addresses are obtained from different sources.

merge/purge. Combining MAILING LISTS and simultaneously de-duplicating since the same names can appear on more than one list. However, if a name is presented or spelt differently it may be difficult to delete duplication.

metallic inks. Those which have metallic powders for printing in gold or silver.

meter advertisements. Advertisements placed on parking meters. They have a repetitive effect on passers-by.

Methuselah market. People within five years of retirement, often with high discretionary income, and special needs regarding housing, financial services, holidays, etc.

metric type sizes. Although the original POINT SYSTEM continues to be used (unlike the replacement of half-tone screens by metric versions), metric type sizes are widely used on the continent and with computerised photo-typesetting or digital typesetting. 1.00mm CH (4pt), 1.50mm CH (6pt), 2.00mm CH (8pt) up to 18mm CH (72pt). CH stands for capital height.

MF. Machine or mill finished paper, calendered to produce smooth finish.

MG. Machine or mill glazed paper with glossy finish on one side. Used for posters.

micro-marketing. Emphasis on advertising and SALES PROMO-TION to sell goods rather than going beyond advertising to rely on price, performance or reputation, wider use of variables being macro-marketing.

microwave television. MVDS method of transmitting TV channels direct to viewers over short range radio links, enabling CABLE TV companies to deliver signals over the last leg of the route to subscriber's home without having to lay extra cable. Could be applied to other TV companies, using high definition digital sound radio, nationally or locally and could then rival cable TV.

middle tones. Mainly in black and white pictures, the grey tones. The finer the half-tone screen, the better the range of tonal values.

milk bottle advertising. Silk-screened advertisements on milk bottles. *See* DOORSTOPPER MILK BOTTLES.

Minicuts. Collection of pages of camera-ready stock artwork, printed on one side, ready for paste-up. Hundreds of pictures in 100 A4 pages. Minicuts, Maidstone.

mini-page. Portrait page advertisement at premium rate filling about three-quarters depth and width of page, with editorial surround.

mining. Seeking new prospects in DIRECT RESPONSE campaign by using large public database. *See also* FISHING, SPELUNKING.

minority viewers. Watchers of high-brow, special interest, or alternative humour etc. TV programmes, mostly late night, BBC2 or Channel 4.

minutage levels. Amount of time permitted for TV commercials, originally decided by IBA but now in a White Paper taken over by Government. *See* BROADCASTING IN THE 90s. Originally, six minutes per hour, usually in two-minute commercial breaks. This was raised to average of seven minutes and then became seven-and-a-half in 1988.

Mirror Group Newspaper Awards. Makes awards such as best use of colour in newspaper advertising and the creative award of excellence.

misleading prices. *See* CONSUMER PROTECTION ACT 1987 and PRICES, MISLEADING.

misredemption. Redemption of SALES PROMOTION coupons for goods other than those being promoted. Some retailers do accept coupons against any purchases provided the promoted product is stocked. Manufacturers attempt to prevent this by printing warnings about malredemption on their coupons. NB: the expression malredemption is sometimes used for mis-redemption, but the latter term is used by Nielsen Clearing House at Corby, which handles redemptions from dealers.

missionary selling. Provision of display material to retailers, sometimes placed by teams of visiting merchandisers. Useful when goods are supplied by wholesalers and there is no direct contact between manufacturers and traders.

Misuse of Drugs Act 1971. Bans offer of a controlled drug, such as in an advertisement.

mix. 1. In films and video, to fade out one image and introduce another. 2. The range of products—the product mix—sold by one manufacturer, e.g. Heinz '57' varieties. *See also* MARKETING MIX.

mnemonic. Set of initials which makes it easier to say or remember series of words, and whereby the initials form a new word. *See* ACRONYM, LASER.

mobile. 1. POINT-OF-SALE display device suspended from ceiling of shop so that it moves with air currents. 2. In some countries, especially Third World, touring film, video or demonstration show. 3. Loudspeaker van or car. 4. Exhibition or hospitality vehicle. 5. Travelling advertising medium such as car, taxi, trailer, van or bus.

mobile advertising. Advertising on vehicles such as vans, buses, cars, taxis or trains. Can display posters where static sites are scarce; has dramatic appeal of movement and can reach succession of audiences. Flexible medium which can be used for short-term promotions such as opening of new store, or to launch new cars.

mock-up. Rough presentation of an idea for print, package, display piece or exhibition stand (which may be a drawing or model).

mod. Modification (of width of type characters, halftones and line art).

modern face. Typeface with vertical thickness to letters such as 'O'.

modular agency. A creative A LA CARTE advertising agency which does no media buying. *See* MEDIA INDEPENDENT.

money refunds. While refunds may be normal in direct response marketing, they are banned under BCAP, Part C, Section 5.8 which says no advertisement for any medicinal product should contain an offer to refund money to dissatisfied consumers.

Monica. CACI's database which predicts likely age group of potential customers according to their first names. CACI claim that 75% of British adult population have a first name which reveals age.

monochrome. One colour, usually black.

monoline. Typefaces, such as SANS SERIF faces, whose strokes are of equal thickness.

monopoly advertisers. Advertisers who take all the available advertising space in or on a medium, e.g. a bus, or whole issue of publication.

monotone. One-colour printing of pictures, usually black.

montage. Artwork made from a combination of pictures.

mood. 1. Advertisement copy which creates an atmosphere, as with many charity advertisements. 2. The mood of reader, viewer or listener at different times of day, or on different occasions, which can effect response to advertising.

mood music. Background music, as in TV and radio commercials, which can enhance appeal of the advertising by being dramatic, modern, romantic and so on.

MOPS. *See* MAIL ORDER PROTECTION SCHEME.

moral rights. An interesting aspect of the COPYRIGHT, DESIGNS AND PATENTS ACT 1988 is Chapter IV on Moral Rights and the right to be identified as author or director. Under Section 77–(1), the author of a copyright literary, dramatic, musical or artistic work, and the director of a copyright film, has the right to be identified as the author or director of the work ... if (2a) the work is published commercially, performed in public, broadcast or included in a cable programme service; or (2b) copies of a film or sound recording including the work are issued to the public. The section goes on to detail other circumstances when identification is now legally required. However, exceptions to the right apply to a computer program, design of a typeface, and any computer-generated work, or when copyright is divested in an employer. A person also has the right not to have a work or film falsely attributed to him.

MOSAIC. Developed in 1986 by CCN, a neighbourhood classification system which defines 58 lifestyle categories. Differs from other systems in that it analyses the country at postcode level (averaging 15 households) rather than at census enumeration district level (averaging 170). Financial information is also incorporated. Has been applied by Interactive Market Systems to show geodemographic profiles of magazines.

motivational research. As pioneered in the USA by Dr Ernst Dichter, clinical type studies using small groups which reveal hidden motives not otherwise revealed by traditional questionnaire-type research. Useful when devising copy themes. For example, some products can be presented as rewards rather than for their qualities.

MPS cleaned. Mailing list which has been cleaned by the MAIL-ING PREFERENCE SERVICE.

Multiple-choice question. One which presents respondent with list and questions such as 'which of the following makes of motor-car do you drive?' Best to rearrange order of lists for different respondents when danger of first and last items becoming favourites.

multiple exposure. 1. Single picture made by superimposing images on others. 2. Extent to which readers see a page in a journal more than once.

multiple pack. *See* JUMBO PACK, BANDED PACK.

musical work. According to the COPYRIGHT, DESIGNS AND PATENTS ACT 1988, a musical work means a work consisting of music, exclusive of any words or actions intended to be sung, spoken or performed with the music.

MVDS. Microwave digital sound. *See* MICROWAVE TELEVISION.

N

Nader, Ralph. American lawyer who has championed consumer rights, his criticism of defective products such as cars, foods and toys, and against pollution, resulting in legislation to protect the consumer. In 1989 Nader was campaigning in Britain to reform the UK's system of civil justice to cut the gap with the USA over levels of compensation for victims of personal injury and various types of accident. Objected to absence of jury in British civil cases except libel, which meant low levels of compensation.

NAE. National Association of Exhibitors.

national brand. Brand which is advertised nationally by the manufacturer, as distinct from a retailer's OWN BRAND or OWN LABEL.

National Exhibition Centre. Britain's largest exhibition centre. Purpose-built with hotels, railway station, near motorway and airport. Birmingham.

national press. Newspapers and magazines with national circulation. May be printed in or near London, but some use contract printers strategically placed throughout country. Special feature of British press; most foreign publishers are regionalised, either because of the size of country (e.g. USA) or because modern countries are federations of states (e.g. Germany, Italy). However, satellites have made national presses possible elsewhere.

National Readership Survey. Conducted by JICNARS representing press, agencies and advertisers. Continuous survey of newspaper and magazine readerships, producing readership figures and profiles. Considers secondary readership as distinct from net sale figures authorised by ABC.

natural break. Period during ITV programme when commercials are shown. Following an agreement by 22 countries, the number of advertising breaks was reduced in 1989 to one break in a film of 45 minutes upward, two in a film of 90 minutes and three in films of 110 minutes or more. Previously, in Britain, there had been three or four breaks an hour which was still far less than in USA. *See* MINUTAGE LEVELS.

naturals. CENTREFOLD SPREAD.

Necci enlarger. Japanese equipment for making full-colour printed enlargements direct from photographs on flexible textiles, vinyls, Formica laminate for interior/exterior displays/posters. Nairn Scanachrome, Skelmersdale.

neckline. White space under a headline.

negative line art. Reversing line drawings white on black. Care has to be taken that fine lines are not so weak they will fill in. Can be done digitally. *See* SCANTEX 2000.

negative setting. Setting parts of whole blocks of text in reversed white on black. Small characters can fill-in and become illegible. Can be dramatic provided not overdone. Legibility weakens with volume or weak second colour. If there is a screened background essential that the screen ruling is fine enough to provide a bold background against which reversed type can be read clearly.

neighbourhood types. *See* ACORN.

Nestapak. Direct mail device from Promotion Impressions. Allows an order or application portion of a one-piece mailshot to be trimmed to a smaller width to enable insertion to an integral envelope without having to fold the form. The form can be pre-inserted in the envelope. Colorgraphic Group, Leicester.

net audience. Total audience for a TV/radio airtime schedule, less duplication.

net names. System used in DIRECT MAIL when MAILING LISTS are rented so that a client pays for at least 85% of names supplied no matter how many names are mailed, but the full rental price if 90–95% of list is mailed. *See also* BRITISH LIST BROKERS ASSOCIATION.

network radio advertising. Radio advertising on all ILR stations, booked in packages of days and times.

network TV advertising. Television advertising on all ITV stations.

new product development. Although few new products survive, companies constantly seek new ones. Specialist advertising agencies plan the total operation whereas normal agencies are usually just presented with the product to advertise, at which stage it can be too late. New product development follows a six-stage model: generation of idea; screening to check whether the idea is compatible with business objectives and resources; business analysis to measure the effect in cost and profit; refinement of technical details including branding, packaging; test marketing; and launch.

news proof. Advertisement proofed on NEWSPRINT.

newscaster. Electronically operated, moving lighted sign, spelling out news items interspersed with advertisements, placed high on building and visible at a distance. Usually sited in city centres and railway terminals.

Newspaper Publishers Association. Trade association of national newspaper and London evening newspaper publishers. Recognises advertising agencies for commission purposes.

Newspaper Society. Trade association of regional newspapers. Recognises advertising agencies for commission purposes.

newsprint. Poor quality absorbent paper made from MECHANICAL PULP and used for printing newspapers.

next-day recall. Advertisement research to test impact and awareness of an advertisement and its content on the day following its appearance. *See* RECALL SURVEY, DAY AFTER RECALL, TRACKING STUDIES.

next matter. Press advertisement position next to editorial material. *See* FACING MATTER.

niche marketing. Marketing, including advertising and retailing, aimed at special MARKET SEGMENT.

Nielsen Regions. The nine regions of England, Scotland and Wales used by A. C. Nielsen Co. Ltd which approximate to ITV areas or combinations of ITV areas. These regions are: London, Anglia, Southern, Wales, West & Westward, Midlands, Lancashire, Yorkshire, Tyne-Tees, Scotland.

Nielsen Retail Audit. Invoices and stocks are audited continuously and usually monthly at a sample of stores representing specific universes (i.e. grocers, chemists and druggists, confectioners/tobacconists/newsagents, cash and carry warehouse, DIY outlets, toy specialists, sports goods specialists). Sample data is expanded to represent the total universe. Nielsen samples pick up 10% of all sales of any particular universe.

Indexes are published showing not only shares of the market held by each brand in each product class, but also changes and trends regarding sales, stocks, deliveries, distribution, out-of-stock, price, rate of sale, for total GB and a variety of shop and regional breakdowns. Nielsen conduct similar surveys in 17 countries. Nielsen Marketing Research, Oxford.

Nielsen Scantrack. A panel of Scanner-equipped stores compiled to produce weekly sales information. Only UK source of weekly sales data. Since all products, even offer packs, have separate BAR CODES, a market report has a very high level of product detail. The panel covers all major grocery multiple groups and Co-ops. Data covers sales volume, value, shares, distribution for total panel. Application: mainly as early warning service, as tracking study through which share or sales trend will become apparent. Nielsen Marketing Research, Oxford.

Nielsen Store Observation Service. Fortnightly audit of 440 outlets covering some 35 groups to measure price and presence of products in-store. Other in-store factors (facings, shelf positions, age of stock, etc.) are also measured. The reports contain average and model price and shop and turnover weighted distribution for all groups individually and consolidated. Data are delivered quickly, two working days after audit, so that a fast and frequent price and distribution monitor is provided. Low entry fee attracts both large and small manufacturers. Reveals whether trade deals are being supported and honoured; success of competitor's deals; how competitive one is on shelf in terms of price, space, promotions; how and where one's products are being displayed. Nielsen Research Services, Oxford.

Nielsen Tops/Frozen Food Service. Tapes of deliveries into *all* outlets of Asda, Bejam, Cordon Bleu, Gateway, Iceland, Morrison, Safeway, Sainsbury and Tesco are collated by Nielsen into market reports, on a four-weekly basis. Weekly data are also available. Data covers delivery volumes, values, price, shares, distribution for total GB, regions and distributed by named account. Nielsen Marketing Research, Oxford.

nixie. Mailing shot returned to sender by Post Office because the addressee is dead, has moved or the mailing shot is wrongly addressed.

noticeability. Impact of advertising on radio and television. *See* IMPACT OF BROADCAST ADVERTISING.

noting and reading research. *See* READING AND NOTING TEST.

NPA. NEWSPAPER PUBLISHERS ASSOCIATION.

NPD. *See* NEW PRODUCT DEVELOPMENT.

number. Single issue of a newspaper or magazine. Special number, Christmas number.

numbers buying. Buying media on basis of quantities, e.g. COST PER THOUSAND, IMPACTS.

numeral. Name or symbol to identify a number.

O

OAA Code of Practice. 10-point set of undertakings approved by 28 members of the OUTDOOR ADVERTISING ASSOCIATION. Clauses include ensurance that PANELS are numbered and display the name of the controlling contractor; the handling of all planning issues that could affect advertisers under the Town and Country Planning legislations; and repairs of any damage or removal of graffiti as soon as practicable.

oblique stroke. A slash (/).

oblong. Landscape-shaped. A booklet or catalogue bound at shorter side.

observational research. Marketing research in which the object of study is observed, as with a PANTRY CHECK or DUSTBIN CHECK or a count of passers-by of poster site. No questionnaire is used. Also called 'covert observation' when group activities are watched.

off air. TV programme received directly off the air as broadcast, not by intermediary means such as cable or tape-recording.

off-peak. Before peak TV viewing times, up to 16.20 Monday to Friday, up to 16.00 Saturday, up to 14.00 Sunday.

off-the-page. Selling off-the-page as when a DIRECT RESPONSE marketer places an offer in the press. Has extended into many fields such as financial services.

off-the-screen sales. DIRECT RESPONSE sales using TV commercials and often computerised acceptance of telephoned orders with credit card facilities. TV company supplies advertiser with print-out of orders received.

offending images. Ones used in advertising which offend certain groups such as feminists, animal lovers, non-smokers, teetotallers, environmentalists and ethnic groups. The Robertson's golliwog caused offence.

Office of Fair Trading. Administers FAIR TRADING ACT 1973 which seeks to stop unfair competition such as monopolistic practices. (*See* COMMISSION SYSTEM.) Deals with consumer trade practice which includes advertising, salesmanship, packaging and methods of payment. Under the Act, the Secretary of State for Prices and Consumer Protection, or Director General of Fair Trading, may refer to Consumer Protection Advisory Committee evidence of a practice considered to be against economic interests of consumers. Orders have resulted from proposals by Director General, e.g. the MAIL ORDER TRANSACTIONS (INFORMATION) ORDER 1976, the Business Advertisements (Disclosures) Order 1977. Under the Misleading Advertisements order 1988, the Director General has power to apply for a court injunction to ban offending advertisements, but expects the complainant to seek self-regulatory control first, e.g. through ADVERTISING STANDARDS AUTHORITY.

Office of Population Censuses and Surveys. Responsible for conducting census and official social surveys. Provides statistics based on data held including many statistical returns such as taxes and licences, unemployment figures, etc.

offset-litho. Lithographic printing using a rotary machine, plate cylinder printing on to blanket cylinder which offsets on to paper. *See* LITHOGRAPHY, WEB-OFFSET-LITHO.

old face, style. Early 17th-century typeface with slanting sides to letters such as 'O'. *See* MODERN FACE.

old-shoe language. Words that are familiar to most people. Copywriter has to avoid using words which provoke mental block because of unfamiliarity. Once reading flow is halted, reader's concentration and interest is lost.

omnibus questionnaire. Questionnaire consisting of sets of questions inserted by different fee-paying sponsors. Complete questionnaire mailed by research company to a recruited CONSUMER PANEL.

on-air testing. After transmission of TV commercial(s) depth interviews are conducted among a recruited sample of house-wives. Or recall testing of an unrecruited sample of housewives.

on-label game. Promotional game involving scratch-off bottle labels patented by Don Marketing. First used by Cinzano.

on-pack leaflets. Fix-a-form labelling/leafletting system, where leaflets are attached to packs. Denny Bros Printing, Bury St. Edmunds.

on-sale date. Date when a publication is on sale at the news-agent. Some monthly journals are on sale during the month before the month on cover. Actual selling date could be import-ant to timing of an advertising campaign. *Radio Times*, *TV Times* are on sale some days before programme listings become effective.

on-screen layouts. Composition of advertisement or page on computer VDU prior to film and plate-making, thereby mak-ing paste-up irrelevant.

on the run. While printing presses are running. In web-offset printing all four colours are printed continuously, or 'on the run'.

on-trade promotions. Sales promotion schemes linked to parti-cular classes of retail trade, e.g. grocers, petrol stations or pubs.

one-off payments. Method of paying an actor a once-and-for-all fee for appearing in a TV commercial, thus avoiding repeat fees or disputes with Equity, the actors union. Some fees have ranged between £25,000 and £75,000.

one-piece mailer. DIRECT MAIL shot complete in itself, either in folder or booklet form. May contain means of refolding and reply, but an envelope is required if payment is to be included other than charge card reference. Typical one-piece mailer folds down from broadsheet, like a map.

one-stage advertising. DIRECT RESPONSE, OFF-THE-PAGE, press advertisement, seeking to sell right away.

one-to-one mailings. DIRECT MAIL method consisting of separate cards for individual advertisers. Cards may be bound together as tear-off cards (like a cheque book) or produced singly and despatched in heat-sealed iron-coated plastic wrappers. ICD Direct, London.

OPCS. *See* OFFICE OF POPULATION CENSUSES AND SURVEYS.

open-ended question. In marketing research questionnaire, a question which is not coded for expected answers, but which invites the respondent to speak freely. Verbatim answer summarised by interviewer.

open rate. In press advertising, highest rate on which discounts are based.

opinion poll or research. Marketing research technique which tests opinion, and change of opinion over time when surveys conducted at regular intervals. May use either QUOTA or RANDOM SAMPLE, which can produce different results for similar enquiries due to greater accuracy of latter. Well-known examples are the National Opinion Poll and Gallup Poll.

opportunities to hear. Number of times a member of a target audience is exposed to a station broadcasting a commercial.

opportunities to see. Originally applied to poster advertising, but has become generally applied to all visual media. With poster and transportation advertising, provides a yardstick similar to cost-per-thousand circulation or readership with the press. London Underground has researched its travelling public and has basis for OTS figures. *See* PEDESTRIAN TRAFFIC FLOW.

opportunity to recall. In radio survey (*see* IMPACT OF BROADCAST ADVERTISING) each individual multiplied by the number of commercials while they were listening/viewing.

optical letterspacing. The way in which an impression of even spacing is created by varying space between letters according to their shape.

opticals. In TV, film and video-making, visual effects created by laboratory processes and camera devices. Fade-ins and fade-outs open and close sequences. Dissolve, or mix, is fade-in or fade-out superimposed on another. Wipe is complete change of picture with no double-image. Matte or mask effects used when pictures taken at different times to make eventual one whole, as when packs or cartoon characters are superimposed on live sequences in commercials. A super is lettering superimposed on a picture, and a pop-on is an optical device for flashing prices, slogans on and off.

opto-mechanical typesetting. After more than 500 years of using metal type, printers were—in the early 60s—able to use a new typesetting technique. A film strip, glass disc or plate replaced hot metal setting. From a master FOUNT any number of characters in desired sizes could be exposed to photographic paper or film. The photographic master was superseded by the digital method in the 70s. By the mid-80s it became possible to output graphic elements and technical screens. *See* SCANTEX 2000.

Oracle. Optical Reception of Announcements by Coded Line Electronics. Owned by INDEPENDENT TELEVISION ASSOCIATION. Provides off-air data display services on ITV, CHANNEL 4, s4c and TV-AM. ITV teletext alphanumeric information system available free-of-charge on sets fitted to receive it (together with BBC Ceefax). Pages on sale to advertisers. Not linked to the telephone, and there is no charge for viewing pages, as with PRESTEL. Information generated by computer, constantly updated, and covers numerous topics such as news, motorway traffic reports, City prices, sports results, etc. Also, encoded teletext Subscription User Group Service (SUGS) for data information of interest to specific sections of the public.

oral satisfaction market. Includes culinary devices such as yoghurt machines, waffle irons, woks, sandwich toasters, automatic juice extractors and Italian ice-cream makers to clutter up Yuppie kitchen.

oramedia. In Third World, non-commercial traditional forms of communication which may, according to part of the world, include: rumour, oratory, poetry, music, singing, the drum, linguists, ornaments, charms and insignia, masks, market gossip, festivals, gongmen or town criers, folk theatre, folk tales, puppet and shadow shows.

order building incentive. Extra or special offer to encourage customer to maximise value of DIRECT RESPONSE order, e.g. gift every time certain order figure is passed.

ordinary position. In press advertising, RUN-OF-PAPER, or no special position.

original. Artwork for reproduction.

ornamented. Typeface with fancy flourishes.

OSCAR. *See* OUTDOOR SITE CLASSIFICATION AND RESEARCH.

OSM. *See* ORAL SATISFACTION MARKET.

OTC. *See* OVER THE COUNTER.

OTH. *See* OPPORTUNITIES TO HEAR, FREQUENCY.

OTR. *See* OPPORTUNITY TO RECALL.

OTS. *See* OPPORTUNITIES TO SEE.

out-of-home media. All media seen outside the home such as cinema, outdoor, transportation and point-of-sale, and exhibitions.

outdoor advertising. Advertising out-of-doors such as posters and signs, other than advertising on transportation vehicles and property.

Outdoor Advertising Association of Great Britain. Represents outdoor advertising industry. Represents 90% of roadside sites but also represents majority of transport contractors. Total expenditure on outdoor advertising (including production) approximately £220m. London. *See* OAA CODE OF PRACTICE, OSCAR, POSTER MARKETING.

Outdoor Site Classification and Research. Poster site database based on information provided by Outdoor Advertising Association, London.

OSCAR data is copyright of the OAA and is developed and maintained by Associated Information Services, a wholly owned computer bureau of National Opinion Polls. Provides analysis of 171 socioeconomic target groups. OSCAR includes all poster panels of 4-sheet size or greater at roadside sites or pedestrian only areas, concerning more than 90% of all such panels in existence in UK. A 100% census conducted by NOP. Visibility adjusted audience data available for every roadside poster panel giving total weekly audience that can see an individual advertisement (= the Opportunity to See).

It is a continuous study, data are available on-line from Associated Information Services Ltd or in hard copy in six-monthly *OSCAR Digest*, published Spring/Autumn. Gross OSCAR audience is estimated by the total number of people passing each site every week, separated into pedestrians/vehicular traffic. Visibility adjusted scores (= OTS) are the basis for buying nett audience for their posters, gross potential audience reduced by allowances for visibility distance, competitive poster panels, angle of panel to sightline, height/deflection, permanent obstruction, illumination (30% increase if lit).

outline. Typeface with only an outline and no solid body.

over matter. Typesetting in excess of available space.

over the counter. (OTC) Referring to branded proprietary medicines as retailed by pharmacists, as distinct from ETHICAL PHARMACEUTICALS.

over-redemption. Excessive response to SALES PROMOTION offers. Sometimes difficult to gauge likely response, and wise to place a limit such as first so many applications. Otherwise embarrassing if apologies necessary. Could be financial loss if excess demand had to be satisfied.

overall painted bus. Bus painted to design of a single advertiser. Available with many private bus companies. It was a common sight in London in 1970s but withdrawn. Confusion possible when routes identified by buses of certain colours.

overhang cover. Book cover larger than pages, as with some bibles with leather covers.

overkill. Result of excessive advertising appeals, when claims or promises defy credibility or methods used, as with some mail shots, are overdone, causing irritation or disbelief.

overspill media. Media which have circulations or audiences extending beyond the original area or country, as with many European newspapers. But particularly relevant to cable and satellite TV.

own brand, label. Goods like coffee, tea, baked beans, packed in name of retailer like Sainsbury's, Tesco. Can be cheaper than NATIONAL BRAND, but may also be of a different quality. May be made to retailer's specification. Means of competing with advertised brands. Some firms, e.g. Nestlé, refuse to supply own brands. Other firms contract packers only and have no national brands. Firms which pack both enjoy more economic volume production.

ozalid. Diazo copying process used for page proofs. *See* BLUES, BLUEPRINTS, DIAZO.

P

p. Page. Plural pp.

PAC. Pinpoint Address Code. *See* GEOPIN.

pack recognition. Linkage between advertising and point-of-sale. If the package is clearly shown in advertising especially where there are opportunities for colour, a customer can seek or recognise it in the store.

package insert. Either 1. A gift as sales promotion scheme, e.g. plastic toys in breakfast cereals; or 2. instruction leaflets or STUFFERS. Also, package outsert attached to exterior. With inserted gifts, it is necessary to take care that they will not contaminate the food product, and if such a risk exists they should be contained in separate bag.

packaging. Way in which a product is packed for protection, as a container, as a means of identifying product, and as a means of advertising it. PACK RECOGNITION is an important link between advertising and POS presentation.

PAF. *See* POSTCODE ADDRESS FILE.

page. 1. On PRESTEL, one or more numbered frames of information. 2. In printing, one side of a leaf.

page make-up. Assembly of text and pictures in a page to complete whole design. Can be done by computer on a VDU.

page proof. Proof resembling eventual printed page, that is with spacing, display lines, and complete as opposed to a run-on galley proof. At this stage corrections must not affect succeeding pages, and only minor ones or ones confined to the page, should be made.

page traffic. Breakdown by SOCIAL GRADE, sex, and other classifications of readership of different pages of a journal. In Gallup NOTING AND READING research detailed scores are given for each page of a publication, with full-page advertisements identified.

page zero, page 0. Top index page of teletext material.

pagination. Contents list of a brochure, catalogue, magazine or newspaper, showing items to appear on each page.

paid sheet. Newspaper or magazine which is retailed and has a COVER PRICE in contrast to a freesheet (FREE NEWSPAPER) or give-away magazine.

paint on film. Method of producing animated films (cartoons), characters and sequence of actions being painted on film by the animator.

Paintbox. Video paint system using Quantel's creative design computer. Alternative to CAD/CAM systems. Images are created with smoothly rounded curves, natural colour mixing, selecting from big range of mediums, brush sizes, yet avoiding computer appearance. Stencil and paste-up functions. Paste over live video facility. *See* QUANTEL, GRAPHIC PAINTBOX, HARRY ANIMATION.

painted bus. *See* OVERALL PAINTED BUS.

paired comparison test. PRODUCT PRE-TEST technique in which respondents compare one product with another. Products may not be identified. *See* BLIND PRODUCT TEST.

PAL. *See* PHASE ALTERNATING LINE.

Palcrypt. French pay-channel encryption system developed by Thomson and News Data Security Products and adopted by SKY CHANNEL, initially for its Sky Movies.

Pan-European Readership Survey. Study of journals circulating throughout Europe. English-language journals predominate.

Pan-European Television Audience Research. Survey for nine satellite TV channels and five media organisations (including IBA) conducted in 11 European countries by Research Services Ltd. Uses diaries completed by 4807 viewers, but plans to install meters like BARB.

pan media. Media such as journals with international circulations or satellite TV which have cross-frontier readerships and audiences.

panel. 1. In outdoor advertising, a poster site. 2. Recruited respondents, often housewives or householders, who provide regular reports on continuous surveys such as consumer panels and BARB TV surveys. Data usually recorded in daily diary. May test products.

Pantone. System of matching colours and choosing printing inks, using numbered colour samples. Pantone Inc. Check-standard trade mark for colour reproduction and colour reproduction materials such as Pantone markers. Marketed UK by Letraset. London.

pantry check. Observational marketing research method. A panel is visited by researchers who record brands in kitchens/bathrooms.

paper set. Advertisement set by a publisher as opposed to the publisher supplied with CAMERA-READY COPY.

paper sizes. ISO sizes are: A1 594 × 841 mm; A2 420 × 594 mm; A3 297 × 420 mm; A4 210 × 297 mm; A5 148 × 210 mm; A6 105 × 148 mm; A7 74 × 105 mm. RA sizes untrimmed. Slightly larger SRA sizes which allow trimming of grip edges and BLEEDS. B sizes in between A sizes for posters and big envelopes. C sizes for envelopes.

paragraph opener. Box symbol to emphasise opening of paragraph.

PASE. On-line availability and booking systems for outdoor advertising, with separate systems for contractors and agencies. Provided by Associated Information Services, London.

pass-on-readership. Secondary readership as when a journal is passed round the office. The *Financial Times* has a small circulation but a large pass-on-readership.

passing-off. Misleading presentation of a package so that it is bought in mistake for a well-known brand. *See* GET-UP. Legal action requires proof that there is probability of confusion in the minds of buyers, and to have caused loss of trade. Apart from packaging, passing-off can be attempted by using a similar name but with a slight change of spelling.

paste-up. Dummy with proofs pasted in position.

paste-up artist. Studio artist who sticks copy in position as camera-ready artwork, but make-up of artwork or pages can be done on computer screen.

pasteboard. Cardboard made of thin sheets stuck together. Ticketboard.

patching. Pasting corrections on to film or artwork before making litho plate.

peak listening hours. Hours when most people listen to the radio. This can vary according to the type of listener, e.g. breakfast time, morning and afternoon (car commuters), mornings (housewives), lunch time, late night (teenagers).

peak point. In cinema advertising, point between feature films when commercials are shown, so that commercials are included in each complete programme. There are no NATURAL BREAKS as with showing of films on TV.

peak viewing hours. Mid-evening when TV attracts largest audience. Begins earlier outside London due to different working hours and earlier arrival home from work. Later on Sundays.

pedestrian housewife poster. Four sheet poster displayed in shopping precincts.

pedestrian traffic flow. Number of people using certain routes. It is used as a measure of OPPORTUNITIES TO SEE poster sites.

peep box. *See* PUPIL RESPONSE.

pelmet. POS display piece stuck to top edge of shop window.

penetration, market. Ability of advertising medium to reach the market, and extent of its REACH. Controlled circulation magazines and free newspapers have great penetration because the circulation is not limited to buyers.

People Meter. AGB's push-button hand-set used with set meter for BARB TV audience research to record number and demographic characteristics of the individuals watching TV. Meters are fitted to TV sets in 3,000 homes (subject to increase under new contract), recording minute by minute, both the state of the set, and by means of hand-set, the above details. Equipment measures viewing through up to four units (TV sets and VCRs) in each home.

per single column centimetre (PSCC). Basic unit for charging for press advertisement space.

perceived image. Current image. External mental image of a company based on knowledge and experience.

percentage of anticipated turnover method. Basing advertising appropriation on sales forecast.

percentage of previous turnover method. Basing advertising appropriation on previous year's turnover, and not allowing for any future increase in sales.

perception gap. Difference between the image a company would like to have, and what the PERCEIVED IMAGE actually is.

perfect binding. Method of binding leaves backs being trimmed and glued to cover. Badly done, leaves can burst free. Used for paperback books, telephone directories. Also called adhesive, cut-back or thermoplastic binding.

perfecting. Printing both sides of a sheet at one pass in a perfector press.

performers, rights of. Under Part 11, Rights in Performances, of the COPYRIGHT, DESIGNS AND PATENTS ACT 1988, rights are conferred on performers and persons having recording rights,

requiring their consent to the exploitation of their performances. An exclusive recording contract means a contract
between a performer and another person under which that
person is entitled to the exclusion of all other persons (including
the performer) to make recordings of one or more of his performances with a view to their commercial exploitation. *See*
ILLICIT RECORDING.

perimeter advertising. *See* ARENA ADVERTISING.

Periodical Publishers Association. Trade association of magazine publishers. Recognises advertising agencies for commission purposes. London.

peripheral media. Small circulation journals of little if not ques-
tionable advertising value.

PERS. PAN-EUROPEAN READERSHIP SURVEY.

personal column. Newspaper column which carries small personal CLASSIFIEDS. If commercial advertisements are placed in
personal column they are usually inserted after genuine personal ads.

personality promotion. Product promotions using personalities
such as trade characters or celebrities, in-store or elsewhere.

personalisation. 1. Use of recipient's name in a sales letter
or other mail shot material. Can be introduced in body of
text by laser printing. Can help to make DIRECT MAIL more
personal, but can be an irritant if over done; 2. Desire to
distinguish oneself from others by the brands bought or shops
used, revealing personal style or status.

PETAR. *See* PAN-EUROPEAN TELEVISION AUDIENCE RESEARCH.

pH. P-descenders which affect body height of a typeface. Their
height from base line. *See also* AH and KPH.

Phase Alternating Line. Standard colour television system used
by most western European countries.

photocomposition. Photoelectronic cold typesetting. Characters are photographed to required size using the same size

master photo-matrix for all type sizes. Direct film positives are introduced at once to imposition and platemaking. Copy held in computer memory, usually on floppy discs, making corrections easy when copy is called up on VDU.

photograph. According to the COPYRIGHT, DESIGNS AND PATENTS ACT 1988, a photograph means a recording of light or other radiation on any medium on which an image is produced or from which an image may be by any means produced, and which is not part of a film. *See* COPYRIGHT OWNERSHIP.

photogravure. Printing process using metal plate or cylinder (sleeve) with cells recessed to depth required by quantity of ink. Used for printing popular magazines, although competition from offset-litho. Good quality gravure used for printing postage stamps, fine art prints. *See also* KLISCHOGRAPH.

photomechanical transfer. Paper negative used to produce positive print by chemical transfer.

photo-offset-lithography. Planographic printing process. *See* OFFSET-LITHO, WEB-OFFSET-LITHO.

pi characters. Typographical characters not found in ordinary alphabet or fount. Special symbols.

pica. 12 points. Typographical measurement.

pictogram. Used to represent volumes of data in round figures or proportions, e.g. a pie chart. Symbols on a chart to represent quantities.

picture cards. Either inserted in or cut from packs, give-away cards which can be collected to form a set. SALES PROMOTION scheme which encourages habit buying. Before the Second World War sets of 50 cards issued by Wills Gold Flake and Players Navy Cut cigarettes which are still collectors' items.

picture sorting. QUALITATIVE RESEARCH method. Respondents sort pictorial material and look for visual references for their feelings. References linked to mood and tone of advertising.

Object to trigger associations most likely to be appealing in advertising. Similarly, music can be selected instead of pictures.

piercing. Extracting rectangle of white space from picture and using space for a caption.

piggybacking. 1. In marketing research, placing a set of questions on a mailed omnibus questionnaire containing questions from various sponsors. 2. In DIRECT MAIL/DIRECT RESPONSE marketing, bounceback, co-op mailing, third-party or swap mailing when a mail shot is inserted with another non-competitive mailing, e.g. gas/electricity/credit card bills. 3. In USA, transporting goods on a railway flat wagon. 4. Sale of extra items such as accessories. 5. American term for joining together two TV commercials.

pilfer-proof cap. *See* ROLL-ON PILFER-PROOF CAP, and TAMPER-EVIDENT, RESISTANT PACKAGES.

pilot market. Test marketing. *See* TEST AREA, TEST MARKETING.

pilot survey. Initial small marketing research survey to test the validity of a questionnaire and feasibility of a full survey.

PIN. *See* PINPOINT IDENTIFIED NEIGHBOURHOODS.

Pinpoint Identified Neighbourhoods. Analyses 130,000 neighbourhoods, identifying 60 types of census neighbourhoods. *See* GEOPIN, FINPIN. Pinpoint software can perform keyword searches on a 23m address Postcode Address File created by the Post Office. Has proprietary computer mapping system which can show output of Pinpoint Analysis by means of location plotting and density shading of areas. Computer maps can be produced as translucent overlays and to any scale. Pinpoint have compressed the entire output of the 1981 census small area statistics on to a single disc. Pack for on-line access.

Pinstripe. Bar code in form of 3in strip holding up to 1,000 characters or can carry a signature and monochrome photograph. Indecipherable to human eye, easily machine-read by special scanner. American system supplied by Pinpoint Analysis Ltd.

pixel. In digital production of screen tints and halftones, the smallest exposable point of the image setter.

placard. Small double-crown poster or bill as used to advertise newspapers outside newsagents shops or by street newsvendor.

planning director. In advertising agency, the head of ACCOUNT PLANNING.

plans board. In some advertising agencies, a committee of departmental heads, chaired by account executive, which discusses new assignments and has meetings to plan strategy before presentation is made to client. *See also* REVIEW BOARD and CREATIVE GROUP.

plate cylinder. In rotary press, the cylinder which carries printing plate.

platform. Copy theme of an advertisement. *See* UNIQUE SELLING PROPOSITION.

playing cards. Give-away advertising medium with advertisement on backs of cards. Artwork, printing by playing card manufacturer, e.g. Carta Mundi, Waddington. *See also* TUCK-BOXES.

plug. Free advertising, e.g. when a product is plugged in the media. Not to be confused with public relations which is concerned with factual information. Consequently, PR material should not be capable of being accused of plugging because company and brand names appear too frequently or obviously.

PMT. PHOTOMECHANICAL TRANSFER.

Point of sale/purchase. Display material supplied by manufacturers to advertise products in shops.

point system. 72 points to the inch, based on Didot's typographical measurement system. Type sizes are stated in points, e.g. 6pt, 12pt, 72pt. 10 on 11 means 1pt spacing between lines.

political advertisements. While not permitted on broadcast media (not to be confused with allocated time for party political broadcasts) permitted in most other media such as press, outdoor and direct mail. Political claims are dealt with under Truthful Presentation, sections 6.1–6.3, Part B, General Rules, BRITISH CODE OF ADVERTISING PRACTICE. All advertisements which contain 'political' claims should be readily recognisable as advertisements, cause no confusion as to the identity or status of the advertiser, and wherever such information is not otherwise readily accessible, state the advertiser's address or telephone number.

poll. Survey of attitudes, awareness, opinions, originated by Mass Observation Poll, also conducted by Gallup Poll and National Opinion Poll.

polythene envelopes. Three kinds: block-headed heat sealable in blocks of 100, with two holes so that filler can attach block to worktop with screws or dowels; wicketed which are bunched in 100s and 250s, have metal U bracket for easy tear-off, and can be used on wrapping machines; and self-seal which are more suitable for hand filling by outworkers.

pop video. As seen in some TV commercials, use of abstract forms in contrast to traditional narrative style.

pop-ons. *See* OPTICALS.

pop-ups. Die-cut effect which allows parts of a piece of print, e.g. mailshot, to physically pop up when opened. Examples are pointing fingers, noses. *See* POPPAGRAPH.

Poppagraph. DIRECT MAIL shot technique whereby a die-cut shaped image stands in relief when a printed item is opened. Can have a dramatic or humorous effect, giving movement to a static piece of print. Colourgraphic Group, Leicester.

population. In marketing research, all the people relevant to an enquiry. In social science, flow of people through time. In census-taking, the total number of people.

portrait. Opposite to landscape, an upright page or picture, vertical sides being longest.

portrait page. *See* MINI-PAGE.

positioning. Aiming a product at an appropriate MARKET SEG-MENT, and addressing the advertising to this segment in the appropriate media.

positive recall rating. In radio survey (*see* IMPACT OF BROADCAST ADVERTISING) percentage of individuals who recall, either prompted or spontaneously, commercials broadcast at times when they were listening/viewing.

Post Office Consumer Panel. Run by RSGB, consists of 1,000 households in which all adults note receipt of mail, which is analysed in 12-week blocks. Typical analysis has shown bias towards DIRECT MAIL being addressed to social grades A and B, and most direct mail received at weekends.

post-production. After a video has been shot, all the additional work such as special sound, music and computer graphics effects, titling and perhaps voice-over necessary to complete video.

post-testing. Method of testing advertising after it has appeared, e.g. READING AND NOTING TESTS, NEXT-DAY RECALL, TRACKING STUDIES.

postal diagnosis. An old racket, this is prohibited by BCAP, Part C. 5.2 which says no advertisement should contain any offer to diagnose, advise, prescribe or treat by correspondence. One dubious advertiser used to ask people to mark where it hurt on a drawing of the human body, and a so-called treatment was supplied for a fee.

postal sector marketing. Particularly effective in DOOR-TO-DOOR DISTRIBUTION, means of selecting households in descending order of target penetration. This might reveal how many potential customers live within easy reach of supplier. Part of Insight service from Credit and Data Marketing Services Ltd, Liverpool. *See* SUPER PROFILES.

postcode. Combination of up to seven alphabetical and numerical characters which define four different levels of geographic unit. There are 120 postcode areas, e.g. CR for Croydon, and these areas are divided into 2,700 districts represented by figure in first half of postcode (e.g. CR2). There are 8,900 sectors. Streets, or parts of streets, are given final two alpha codes. Complete postcode: CR2 7LA. There are 1.5m postcodes covering 22m addresses. Some 170,000 addresses which receive heavy mail are given Large User Postcodes, other Small User Postcodes. Each postcode is shared by about 15 addresses. Greatly help speedy sorting and delivery, and can also help locate an incorrect address. Postcodes should always be given in business addresses, and requested on coupons.

Postcode Address File. Royal Mail listing of every address and postcode for every address in Britain, totalling more than 23.5m addresses. PAF is available in directories and on microfiche, magnetic tape and disc. The Post Office supplies labels in combinations of postcodes as required.

postcode maps. Scale maps showing postcode district boundaries, published by John Bartholomew, Geographia Ltd, and Postcode Marketing, Postal HQ, London.

poster. One of the oldest forms of advertising. Printed advertisement bill pasted on various kinds of poster site, or displayed elsewhere such as in windows and shop displays. Some, like Guinness', have become collector's pieces. They have great power—because of size, position, colour, repetition—to be remembered for very long time. Once called 'The Poor Man's Art Gallery'.

Poster Marketing. 1986. Marketing arm of OUTDOOR ADVERTISING ASSOCIATION by which it is funded. Promotes the poster industry on behalf of poster contractors. Publishes quarterly *Poster Scene*. London.

Poster Marketing Effectiveness Awards. Annual contest organised by POSTER MARKETING. Case histories on winning campaigns are available from Poster Marketing. Winners receive a trophy, £1,000, with a feature in *Campaign*. Overall winner receives £10,000 of free poster space.

Poster Payments Clearing House. Set up by IPA and OAA in 1989, processes outdoor space payments so that agencies pay contractors direct to protect their principality, with a commission structure of 15% plus 5%. The 5% specialist commission is paid by the clearing bank, on behalf of the contractors, as soon as the agency pays the Clearing House. Poster contractors fund Clearing House.

poster research. *See* OSCAR.

poster showing. Assortment of outdoor poster sites rented as a package. Number of posters based on the number estimated to reach a given audience, 100, 50 or 25 showing.

poster sizes. 4 sheets = 5ft × 3ft 4ins; 12 sheets = 5ft × 10ft; 16 sheets = 10ft × 6ft 8ins; 48 sheets = 10ft × 20ft; 64 sheets = 27ft × 10ft; 96 sheets = 40ft × 10ft. Unit sheet size is double crown (small billboard/window bill/placard size). Quad Crown is often used for small posters advertising entertainments, e.g. walls of Underground, British Rail stations. Posters are not printed in 'sheets' of the above sizes: the term 'sheets' is simply one of measurement.

postscript. Some DIRECT MAIL exponents believe a P.S. attracts attention, can be used to win extra interest and can add a valid sales argument. But condemned by others who consider it a childish device, making a sales letter look amateurish or descend into OVERKILL. Best avoided, if it detracts from credibility.

potential audience. In TV advertising, potential audience of any defined audience group is the total defined audience group within HOME ITV HOMES for any ITV region, or within ITV Homes for an ITV region, or within ITV Homes for the ITV network as a whole.

pp. Pages.

PPA. PERIODICAL PUBLISHERS ASSOCIATION.

PPI. *See* PRINTED POSTAGE IMPRESSIONS.

pre-empt system. Much criticised method of selling TV airtime subject to latest bid, making it impossible to plan spots economically. Whereas an advertiser cannot cancel within six to eight weeks, contractors can cancel if they are offered better price.

pre-print. Part of print-job run off in advance, as sometimes occurs with colour pages in newspapers, especially when colour pages pre-printed by a different process. Part-printed reels fed into press for black and white printing.

pre-test. 1. Trial run of direct mail shot. 2. Pre-test of different prices for direct response offer to see which price wins best response. 3. ADVERTISEMENT PRETESTING, FOLDER TECHNIQUE, IN-THEATRE RESEARCH, PRODUCT PRE-TEST to get people's reactions to new product.

Precision Marketing. Weekly news magazine of direct marketing. London. 1988.

prelims. First pages of a book preceding the text and containing details of title, contents, copyright and printing history.

premium offer. Goods offered at special price in return for voucher, label, wrapper, token or packet top and cash. Self liquidating since no profit made by advertiser, but costs covered. Important to warn that delivery may take 21–28 days. Product may not be available in shops so the evaluation of likely retail price must be fair. However, premium offers are less popular than offers which can be redeemed without having to write away.

presentation. 1. The way an advertisement is set out. Its use of layout, typography, illustration. Presentation of copy. 2. The way a proposed advertising campaign is explained and demonstrated by the agency to the client.

presenter. Actor or celebrity who makes the sales pitch in a TV or radio commercial.

presort. In direct mail, the sorting of mailing shots by postal town, to earn Post Office rebate on presorted bulk mail. *See* MAILSORT.

press advertising. Advertising in print media, e.g. newspapers, magazines, catalogues, programmes, directories, yearbooks.

pressure-sensitive labels. Self-adhesive labels, in roll-feed form for labelling machines.

Prestel. 1979. British Telecom's alphanumeric viewdata TV information system. TV set has to be modified to receive pages transmitted from a computer via the telephone line. Advertisers can buy pages. Viewers pay for pages called up. Not on-air or free-of-charge to viewer like ORACLE

prestige advertising. *See* INSTITUTIONAL ADVERTISING.

price band. Price level of a group of similar products, usually selling to particular MARKET SEGMENT.

Price Marketing (Bargain Offers) Order 1979. Goods sold at a reduced price must have previously been on sale at the higher price. If a store has many branches, the address of a branch selling goods at higher price should be stated. Some press ads have caused offence because the price reduction was obscure, the full price having been charged at only one store and then only a legal get-out when supposedly reduced price is actually the normal price. Dubious pricing by certain stores which hold perpetual 'sales'.

price promotions. All those SALES PROMOTION schemes which involve price-cuts, e.g. FLASH PACKS, BANDED PACKS, cash premium vouchers, coupon books, etc. The reduction is usually equivalent of expenditure on advertising. Advertiser 'spends' advertising appropriation in form of price cut.

Prices Act 1974. Regulations made under this Act call for clear marking of prices of certain goods. Retailers are required to display information about the range of prices at which goods are normally sold. One regulation applies to the display of petrol prices, although it is no longer necessary to do so in gallons as well as litres.

prices, misleading. Under the Consumer Protection Act 1987, an indication given to any consumers is misleading as to price if . . . (a) the price is less than in fact it is; (b) the applicability of the price does not depend on facts or circumstances on which its applicability does in fact depend; (c) the price covers matters in respect of which an additional charge is in fact made; (d) a person who in fact has no such expectation (i) expects the price to be increased or reduced (whether or not at a particular time or by a particular amount); (ii) expects the price, or the price as increased or reduced, to be maintained (whether or not for a particular period); and (e) the facts or circumstances by reference to which the consumers might reasonably be expected to judge the validity of any relevant comparison made or implied by the indication are not what in fact they are. The Act continues with two more sections concerning what constitutes misleading pricing.

primary colours. In printing inks, yellow, magenta (red) and cyan (blue). In light, red, green and blue.

primary media. In an advertising campaign, the main media which spearhead a campaign. Other media are secondary or support media. The choice depends on the type of advertiser and campaign. For a FMCG advertiser, primary media could be press or TV; for an industrial advertiser, primary media could be the trade press or a trade exhibition; for a DIRECT RESPONSE (mail order) advertiser primary media could be direct mail and catalogues.

primary offer. In DIRECT RESPONSE marketing, the chief offer, although a catalogue or advertisement may include other or alternative offers.

primary research. New, original marketing research as distinct from existing, published secondary research material such as Government statistics.

prime time. Most expensive ITV airtime because audiences are at their largest. PEAK VIEWING airtime.

print run. Total number of copies printed.

Printed Postage Impressions. Pre-printed alternative to postage stamps and frankings, providing ready-stamped envelopes or labels. This service is explained and specimen designs can be found in a booklet *Printed Postage Impressions* from the Royal Mail. Can be pre-printed by customer's own printer.

privacy in photographs, films. Under Section 85 of the COPYRIGHT, DESIGNS AND PATENTS ACT 1988, a person who for private and domestic purposes commissions the taking of a photograph or the making of a film has, where copyright subsists in the resulting work, the right not to have (a) copies of the work issued to the public, (b) the work exhibited or shown in public, or (c) the work broadcast or included in a cable programme service.

private label. *See* OWN LABEL.

prize draws. Popular form of SALES PROMOTION which developed in late 1980s. No purchase or proof of purchase is necessary. The public is invited to enter for free prize draws organised by an advertiser. Quite different from COMPETITIONS which require proof of purchase as entry requirement, and element of skill as legal requirement. *See* PROMOTIONAL GAMES.

PRN. Pinpoint Road Network. *See* GEOPIN.

probability ranking. Method of DE-DUPLICATING the MAILING LISTS and DATABASES. Instead of de-duping exact matches exclusively it matches names and addresses according to probability ranking. Two similar addresses, though partly different, are not ignored merely because they are not perfect matches. The probability that two slightly different addresses are the same is ranked on a sliding scale. Market Location of Leamington market software as Super Search.

probability sample. *See* RANDOM SAMPLE.

process colours. The four colours used to produce full-colour print: yellow, magenta, cyan and black.

product. Anything that is capable of forming the subject matter of an advertisement. It is most often a tangible object of trade, but may also be, for example, a service or facility, an idea, a cause or an opportunity. (BCAP).

product, cash. One on which no money is spent to advertise or promote it.

product, inside-out, outside-in. Inside-out products are created by a manufacturer, e.g. ready-made clothes. Outside-in products are created by a customer, e.g. custom-made clothes. There is a trend towards customisation and away from mass-production, as seen with motor-cars with individual body finishes.

product line. Family of products sold through same outlets to similar customers, e.g. DIY products, gardening aids, pet foods, fats, canned foods.

product-line enhancement. Association between manufacturer's products so that one helps to sell others: e.g. books in series, varieties of chocolate bar, range of soups. Or accessories like additional lenses for cameras.

product-line pricing. Pricing policy which encourages either stocking or buying of related products, thus compensating for substitution. May be in trade terms or retail prices.

product-line promotional pricing. Occurs when the sale of one line is dependent on the sale of another, e.g. computer hardware and software, razors and blades. Sometimes the basic product cheap, main sales depending on supplies to make it work.

product manager. *See* BRAND MANAGER.

product mix. Range of products made by one manufacturer (or stocked by retailer). Typical example: range of Dulux paints.

product placement. Payment to TV companies and film-makers to include products or advertisements such as shop signs in their productions.

product positioning. Deciding segment of the market most likely to produce sales. This may require finding a gap in the market, and using media aimed at this segment.

product pre-test. Testing of new products to measure acceptance rate or in order to make refinements. May be done with a CONSUMER PANEL, by door-step invitations, by placing the prototype with typical customer, or by using independent test laboratory. *See* PAIRED COMPARISON TEST, BLIND PRODUCT TEST.

product surround. Attributes which increase the value of a product and which can provide selling points in advertising, e.g. delivery reputation or service, after-sales service, re-sale value, cash refunds, testimonials, CORPORATE IMAGE.

production. Creation of advertising materials such as camera-ready copy for publishers.

production department. In an agency or in-house advertising department, the section which both maintains progress chasing, production of advertising materials such as typesettings, and despatches copy to the publisher to meet copy date. Also handles the arrival of proof and despatch of corrections. Sometimes called traffic department.

production manager. In an advertising agency or in-house advertising department, the person responsible for the PRODUCTION DEPARTMENT. Often combines duties of progress chaser and print buyer.

profile. Breakdown of the readership of a publication by SOCIAL GRADE, age groups, sex, occupations, interests and geographical distribution.

progressive graduated screens. In addition to LINEAR GRADUATED SCREENS, shadow effects can be simulated by means of a progressive graduated screen running into a light tone. The graduation of tone shows no visible join and is useful for screened background effects. Horizontal and vertical graduations can be achieved of different lengths, by means of digital typesetting. *See* SCANTEX 2000.

progressive proofs. Proofs pulled from each colour plate, in sequence and building up to full-colour.

projective test. In MOTIVATIONAL RESEARCH, a clinical test which establishes the personality of a respondent. This can then be related to the kind of answer given in other tests.

proliferation. Excessive number of lines or brands, which may be rationalised to eliminate least profitable ones.

promotion. Loose expression for methods of promoting or selling goods and services, e.g. selling, advertising, sales promotion.

promotional clothing. Body media such as T-shirts, sweatshirts, hats, visors, ties and other clothing bearing promoter's name or logo, given away (but sometimes sold). Often associated with sponsorship.

promotional games. Prize contests and games used as sales promotion games. *See* SCRATCH CARDS. Some lucky number, fruit machine, or bingo games. To comply with gaming law, purchase of the product is not essential, as with free entry in prize draws.

promotional mix. The mix or combination of ABOVE-THE-LINE and BELOW-THE-LINE advertising which makes up an advertising campaign.

prompt. In a marketing research survey, a means of producing a respondent's answers such as list of pre-coded answers (MULTIPLE-CHOICE QUESTION) or aided recall cards showing MASTHEADS of titles as used in NATIONAL READERSHIP SURVEY.

prompt card. *See* AIDED RECALL.

proof of purchase. In SALES PROMOTION, means of proving qualification for offer or contest entry such as a token cut from
pack.

proof or pull. Proof of an advertisement or piece of print, 'pulled
up' on a proofing press.

propaganda. Means of gaining support for an opinion, cause
or belief. Not to be confused with advertising or PUBLIC RELA-
TIONS. The misleading expression 'trade propaganda' is sometimes used for advertising in the trade press, or by means such
as direct mail to distributors.

proportion, law of. Pleasant arrangement of layout so that elements are in proportion to one another. Also, sizes of sheets
of paper, print, type areas, margins, pleasantly proportioned,
rectangular rather than square, more space at the foot than
on other three sides.

proposition. A scheme setting out ideas and costs, as with a
proposed advertising campaign presented by agency or consul-
tant to client. *See* PRESENTATION.

prospect. A possible customer. In DIRECT MAIL a MAILING LIST
is a list of prospects or prospective customers.

prospect scoring model. *See* MAILING RESPONSE ANALYSIS.

PRR. *See* POSITIVE RECALL RATING.

PSCC. *See* PER SINGLE COLUMN CENTIMETRE.

psychodrawing. Psychodoodle. Research method requiring
respondents to draw stick men, caption cartoons, or fill in
thought bubbles in drawings. Releases spontaneous responses.
Form of MOTIVATIONAL RESEARCH.

psychographic types. *See* all: BABY BOOMERS; BABY BUSTERS; BUP-
PIES; CRINKLIES; CRUMBLIES; DINKIES; GLAMS; GREY PANTHERS;
GUPPIES; HOLIDAY JUNKIES; JOLLIES; LOMBARD; MANAGING MUMS;
MARKAS; METHUSELAH MARKET; SILVER MARKET; UPPIE; WHAN-
NIES; WOOPIES; WRINKLIES; YUPPIES.

psychographics. Attitudes and behaviour responsible for purchase and use of a product, and choice of brand.

psychography. Study of buying motives. *See* PSYCHOGRAPHIC TYPES.

psychological price. 1. Price which appears to be either a bargain, or cheaper than it really is, e.g. £99 instead of £100. 2. Price which appeals to vanity or status, usually a high price.

public access. PRESTEL terminal available to those who pay for pages through their telephone account, unless pages may be called up free of charge. Other terminals for private use, e.g. companies using Prestel internally.

public affairs. Form of PUBLIC RELATIONS more concerned with corporate, political and financial affairs of a company than with products or services. An American concept, and separation of public affairs and public relations considered to be artificial by those who prefer to unite both under single term 'public relations'.

public information panel. Panel carrying double-crown posters, usually mounted on tubular frames on pavement or in shopping centres or public transport premises.

public relations. Public relations practice is the planned and sustained effort to establish and maintain goodwill and mutual understanding between an organisation and its publics (Institute of Public Relations). Public relations is the art and social science of analysing trends, predicting their consequences, counselling organisation leaders, and implementing planned programmes of action which will serve both the organisation's and the public interest (The Mexican Statement). The first is the IPR definition, the latter, broader definition resulted from a PR conference in Mexico City. Public relations is not to be confused with either ADVERTISING or PROPAGANDA. It applies to the total organisation, internally, externally, commercial or non-commercial. The basic purpose is to create understanding, which can help to make advertising more effective. Unlike advertising where most is conducted by agencies, only about 50% of PR is conducted by consultancies due to greater in-house nature and requirements of PR.

publication. (*v*) When published. (*n*) A newspaper or magazine. From the Latin verb publicare, meaning to seize for public use.

publicity. Another loose term like promotion. Strictly speaking, good or bad result of making known over which there is little control. But used as synonym for advertising and wrongly for public relations, and 'publicity manager' is used as superior title for 'advertising manager'. However, in some activities a publicity manager may seek publicity rather than use advertising, e.g. in holiday resort.

publics. In public relations the groups of people that a PR programme is planned to reach. Likely to be many more publics that the TARGET AUDIENCES or MARKET SEGMENTS at which advertising is aimed.

publisher. In publishing, the person responsible for ordering, printing and distributing copies. May also be responsible for promotion and profitability.

puff, puffery. Old name for advertising, still used by editors, especially when a news release is not limited to facts and resembles an advertisement.

pull. *See* PROOF.

pull-out. Section or supplement in a publication which can be pulled-out. Often used for special numbers of publications, and as means of selling extra advertisement space, e.g. gardening, travel, Christmas gifts.

pull-push strategy. Use of ABOVE-THE-LINE media to pull sales, and POS material or SALES PROMOTION schemes to push sales in a pull through, push through process.

pulsation method. Heavy advertising, followed by a pause, followed up by further burst of intensive advertising.

punch-out. Cut out in print by means of DIE-CUTTING.

pupil response. Marplan research technique in which informant looks into a peep box at a screen which shows a back-projected picture or video. The left eye is photographed to measure the size of the pupil. Afterwards the pictures are studied frame by frame and the size of the pupil is compared with the size when looking at neutral control stimulus.

puppets. Used in TV commercials instead of actors or animation, or in conjunction with them, or with products.

Q

Q-Typeset. System for producing typeset output on to a laser printer. Wide choice of font types, style and sizes. Quadratone Systems (UK) Ltd, London.

QTV. Mounted screens that play video advertisements to queuing customers. Operated by the Post Office in main post offices, or other premises, with take-away leaflets on display. Operates nationally.

quad. Sheet of paper four times standard size, e.g. quad crown poster.

qualifying questions. Questions which identify the relevance of a respondent to a survey, e.g. 'Did you watch television last night?'

qualipop. Newspaper like Eddie Shah's original *Today* which was neither heavy nor popular, appealing to middle-class England.

qualitative. Information in the form of reasons, opinions, motives as produced by MOTIVATIONAL RESEARCH, DISCUSSION GROUP research or intensive unstructured interview.

qualitative research. Marketing research which obtains information based on reasons, opinions or motives by means of clinical tests, in-depth interviews, group discussions. The findings are not represented numerically or in percentages as with QUANTITATIVE RESEARCH.

quality newspapers. Heavies such as *The Times*, *Financial Times*, *Daily Telegraph*, *Sunday Telegraph*, *Sunday Times*, *The Observer*. These have smaller circulations than popular newspapers and tabloids.

Quantel. Makers of PAINTBOX.

quantification or ideal method. Way of basing advertising appropriation on advertising agency proposals for the most effective campaign to achieve target. What it will cost to achieve assignment.

quantitative. Information in the form of numbers, percentages, sterling or other monetary value.

quantitative research. Marketing research in which results are processed numerically or in percentages.

quarter-dot screen. Method used to create a semi-halftone effect when a tonal picture is to be reproduced on rough paper such as newsprint. Achieves increase in quality of fine detail reproduction: e.g. photograph of a motor-car. Quarter-dot technique differs from FULL-DOT since a dot is made up of four quarter circles, each of which can reproduce an individual tone value.

quarto. Original manuscript and letterheading size (10ins × 8ins, 254mm × 203mm) and magazine size (crown 4to). Quarter of a sheet of such paper.

questionnaire. Set of questions used for structured interview in marketing research survey.

questions. *See* CLOSED ENDED, CONTROL, DICHOTOMOUS, DOUBLE-BARRELLED, LOADED, MULTIPLE-CHOICE, OPEN-ENDED, SEMANTIC DIFFERENTIAL. A marketing research questionnaire usually has various styles of questions, both to obtain particular kinds of information and to avoid monotony.

quire. Twentieth part of a ream, or 25 sheets of paper. Newsagents usually buy publications in quires.

quota sample. In marketing research, a sample of respondents found by the interviewer to conform with requirements to interview quotas or numbers of people of prescribed characteristics such as SOCIAL GRADES, sex, marital status. Less expensive but less reliable than RANDOM SAMPLE.

quotes. Inverted commas. Many publishers use single quotes.

R

radio audience. 70 million sets in UK; 97.2% of UK households have a portable domestic radio; 60.8% a clock radio; 63.6% have a radio/cassette recorder; 61.8% have either a car radio or a car radio/cassette player. Source: BREMA. *See* SPLIT-FREQUENCY regarding ILR audiences.

Radio Authority. National authority to oversee radio broadcasting.

Radio Marketing Bureau. Marketing arm of UK independent radio industry. Publishes RADIO THE FACTS.

radio ratings. REACH as a percentage of the population group being measured, which can be all people or any demographic group.

radio sponsorship. *See* SPONSORED RADIO.

Radio The Facts. Booklet containing statistics on independent radio audiences and advertisers published by RADIO MARKETING BUREAU.

ragged right. Unjustified right-hand edge to column or page of typesetting. Can be effective for small items of text, such as simulating readers' letters, but is irritating and difficult to read if overdone.

random sample. As used in marketing research, in which every member of UNIVERSE or POPULATION has an equal chance of being selected. Not really random but very precise. An interval or probability sample. Names and addresses (every *nth* name) are chosen at regular intervals from a list such as the electoral roll or a membership list. Gives a cross-section of population. By law of averages, and because it is not subject to human error, more accurate than a quota sample. Interviewer required to make at least three attempts to locate a respondent before using a replacement. This, and more scattered location of respondents, makes random sample more expensive than quota sample. Used for NATIONAL READERSHIP SURVEY.

range. 1. Align type. 2. Variety of goods in the PRODUCT MIX.

range advertisements. In a MEAL report, these are advertisements in which more than one brand appears in a single advertisement and the total cost of the insertion is divided pro rata to each of the brands advertised.

rate-card. Media owner's list of prices with all the necessary information required by advertiser or agency such as production details and copy date. Reproduced in BRITISH RATE AND DATA.

rate protection. When a new rate-card is issued, existing media bookings are honoured at originally agreed rate.

rateholder. Smallest size advertisement accepted for discounts. Must appear within stated time.

reach. The number of different people who are exposed to an advertising campaign. Also, the ability of a medium to reach a certain audience. *See* FREQUENCY, SHARE OF AUDIENCE, CUMULATIVE AUDIENCE.

reader advertisement. One presented as if it were editorial. Disliked by editors. Publishers usually distinguish by adding words at top such as 'Advertisement' or 'Advertiser's Announcement' which minimises the intended effect. Some reader advertisements are special features, often illustrated with sketches.

reader service. Publisher's service to both readers and advertisers, encouraging a response without the readers having to clip coupons or write to advertisers. Coupon or cards are printed in magazine and readers only have to complete and return them to publishers. In case of free holiday brochures, request may be restricted to 4–6 to avoid wasteful applications.

readership. Those who read a publication, including secondary readership. The readership figure is likely to be at least three times that of the circulation figure based on net sales. *See* READERSHIP SURVEY.

readership survey. Study of those who read a newspaper/magazine, which could be members of a family, people at work, visitors to libraries, people in waiting rooms or at hairdressers' and not just original buyers or recipient. First readership survey conducted by ISBA in the 30s. The Hulton Readership Survey in the 50s was succeeded by an independent National Readership Survey conducted by JICNARS. Also, surveys conducted by individual publishers.

reading and noting test. Sometimes stated in reverse order. Method of testing published advertisements for recall and impact. Respondents are questioned on each component of an advertisement, percentage ratings being collated for men and women readers for each component. An advertisement may be run in a regional edition of national newspaper and, as a result of test, it may be amended before it is run nationally. Can also be applied to evaluation of parts of a newspaper, on behalf of publisher. Conducted in UK by Social Surveys (Gallup Poll) Ltd.

real colour. A single selected colour as distinct from colours produced by process colour printing (cyan, magenta, yellow and black). *See* HKS COLOURS and PANTONE.

ream. Set of 500 sheets of paper, but under metrication also the 1,000-sheet ream.

rear-illuminated Tube car panels. London Underground advertising sites in carriages. Can be on paper or 125 micron photographic film (e.g. Kodak Duratrans). For improved display, posters can be printed in reverse on the back.

rebate rates. Discount or refund paid to advertisers by publisher when new publication fails to achieve circulation on which original rates were based. *See* GUARANTEED CIRCULATION.

rebate sorting. In direct mail, mail pre-sorted to geographical areas to qualify for Post Office discounts on bulk mailings. *See* new system MAILSORT.

rebating of commission. Advertising agencies receive commission on media purchases, but in order to charge fees based on time and expertise this commission may be rebated by charging a client net rates, i.e. less commission.

recall. 1. Product recall. When a fault has been discovered in a product, and it is recalled by appeals to customers who have purchased the faulty product. 2. Aided recall. As in readership surveys, when informants are shown mastheads (titles) of publications. 3. Day after recall. When readers/viewers are questioned the next day to measure what is recalled or remembered of advertisements/commercials if they have been seen by those questioned, usually in street interviews.

recall survey. Survey with no AIDED RECALL. Used for next-day surveys, usually in the street, to test recall of press or TV advertisements. *See* DAY AFTER RECALL, TRACKING STUDIES.

reclosable pack. Pack which can be closed after use and also retained for other uses, e.g. screw-top jar compared with jam jar.

recognition of advertising agencies. For purpose of claiming commission from media owners, recognition is granted by bodies representing media (e.g. NPA, NS, PPA, ITVA, AIRC). Two requirements: agency must have credit worthiness (in order to pay media bills promptly), and must accept the British Code of Advertising Practice. Media bodies do not guarantee rate of commission, which is negotiable between agencies and media owners. Current practice follows monopoly ruling of Office of Fair Trading in 1979, under Restrictive Trade Practices Act 1976.

recognition survey. Form of advertisement research in which recall of press, radio, TV advertisements is measured by READING AND NOTING, NEXT-DAY RECALL, TRACKING STUDY and other tests.

recognition test. Survey to measure the recognition of advertisements with obscured or removed names.

recommended retail price. Not a fixed price. Often referred to as the list price, which may be discounted.

recruitese. Euphemisms used in staff recruitment advertisements which usually mean the opposite or gloss over unattractive aspects, e.g. 'flexible hours' for no payment for overtime.

recto. Right-hand page.

redemption. Trading-in gift vouchers, money-off vouchers, premium coupons or stamps. *See* OVER-REDEMPTION, MALREDEMPTION, MISREDEMPTION.

redemption, instant. On-the-spot redemption of SALES PROMOTION offer, as when gift is given with purchase and application does not have to be mailed in.

redemption rate. Rate at which SALES PROMOTION offers such as money-off vouchers are redeemed at the retailers.

reel. Web or roll of paper used on rotary printing machines.

Reeves, Rosser. Originator of UNIQUE SELLING PROPOSITION in his book *Reality in Advertising*, McGibbon & Kee, 1961.

Regional Newspaper Advertising Bureau. Merged Evening Newspaper Advertising Bureau and Weekly Newspaper Advertising Bureau. Represents and promotes advertising in regional morning, evening, weekly, Sunday newspapers and their related free newspapers. London. 1980.

regional press. Newspapers which do not have national circulations, serving provincial areas of the country.

regional raft. A collection of SALES PROMOTION schemes which can be adopted by distributors in different parts of the country.

register. Correct printing of sequence of colours so that the final effect is sharp, not blurred as when colours are out of register. Correct alignment of pages with consistent margins.

register marks. In colour printing, marks for the correct positioning of paper.

registered designs. The Registered Designs Act 1949 was amended by Part IV, Registered Designs, of the COPYRIGHT, DESIGNS AND PATENTS ACT 1988. Under the Act design means features of shape, configuration, pattern or ornament applied to an article by any industrial process, being features which in the finished article appeal to and are judged by the eye (with certain exceptions). NB: this definition in Part IV, Registered Designs, Section 265 differs from the definition in Part III, 213 — *see* DESIGN. Ownership is similar to that for DESIGN RIGHT but the duration of right is less, five years in the first instance, but this can be extended for a second, third, fourth and fifth period of five years.

registered trade names. Registered names which are entitled to capital initial name such as Pop rivets, Tannoy, Vaseline, but not generic names like aspirin, cornflakes or petrol. Quarterly feature in the *UK Press Gazette*, London.

Registrar-General's Standard Regions. The following geographical regions of Great Britain: North, Yorks/Humberside, East Midlands, East Anglia, South East (Greater London, Rest of SE), South West, West Midlands, North West, Wales, and Scotland. Population (OPSS Population Estimates 1988) 55,355,000. Population of Northern Ireland 1,575,000.

regular ITV viewers. *See* WEIGHT OF VIEWING.

reiteration. One of the most powerful devices in advertising. The repetition of names, slogans, selling points and the repetition of advertisements themselves, especially in regular positions.

release form. As signed by models or others being photographed, filmed or videotaped, giving permission for a picture to be used in advertising.

repeat fees. Controversial subject concerning fees to actors when commercials are repeated. Has been the subject of an agreement between IPA and Equity. High repeat fees can deter advertisers from repeating commercials in minority programmes. Present system relates fees to number of transmissions. Argued that fees should relate to audience size which will cause a problem in 1992. *See* ONE-OFF PAYMENTS.

repetitive question. In a research questionnaire, question asked in different way to check whether the same answer is forthcoming. Clarifies possible misunderstanding and checks accuracy of response.

reproduction fee. Fee payable to copyright owner for publication of photograph, cartoon or other artwork which may be supplied by, say, photo agency or photo library.

requested circulation. With CONTROLLED CIRCULATION magazines ABC certification requires evidence of requested circulation, usually based on return of request cards inserted in magazines.

residual. *See* REPEAT FEES.

residual of previous year's surplus method. Way of taking the following year's advertising APPROPRIATION out of the previous year's profits, instead of more correctly relating the appropriation to the cost of achieving future sales.

resolution. Efficiency of photo-chemical or computer system in reproducing fine detail, hence expression 'high resolution'.

response handling. Services offered by media to encourage and handle response to advertising, especially on TV, e.g. British Satellite Broadcasting offer such a service to DIRECT RESPONSE advertisers. BSB package includes on-screen phone number on the ad. Respondents receive information by phone or mail.

Response Pak. Patented sealed ONE-PIECE MAILER from Promotion Impressions. Produced from a pre-printed sheet incorporating personalisation and other variable data by INK-JET PRINTING. Package opens out to deliver the sender's message in a logical easy-to-read sequence, and includes an outer envelope, introductory letter, brochure or application form and a reply device. Colourgraphic Group, Leicester. *See also* COMPO MAILER.

response trigger. Especially in DIRECT MAIL, a device or gimmick which provokes response such as a COIN RUB, FRAGRANCE APPLICATION, LATEX SILVER SCRATCH OFF, a sealed item with perforated tear-off strip, or RUB AND REVEAL PANELS.

retail audit. *See* DEALER AUDIT.

retailer. Distributor who buys at wholesale prices and sells at retail prices. Usually a shopkeeper.

retailing without stores. Shopping without shops. DIRECT RESPONSE.

retention time. Length of time an advertising message can be retained. Some advertising, such as press and direct mail, can be kept permanently, whereas cinema, radio and TV are ephemeral. Posters enjoy repetitive seeing.

retouching. Improving a photograph so that it reproduces better, e.g. by strengthening highlights, painting out blemishes, backgrounds.

reverse indents. First few characters of paragraph not indented, but all succeeding lines of paragraph indented.

reverse out. Printing white lettering on black or other colour background. If the background is not sufficiently dark or solid, white lettering loses its legibility. The reversed lettering should be large, and there should be little of it, otherwise legibility will be poor.

review board. In an advertising agency, a group which reviews critically work of another group. *See* PLANS BOARD, CREATIVE GROUP.

revise. Further proof of printing, corrections having been made.

rhythm, law of. In layouts, pictures or other artwork, the eye should be encouraged to travel naturally through elements of design.

riding the showing. Either viewing outdoor advertising sites for a proposed poster campaign, or inspecting such sites.

ring papers. In continental Europe, newspapers like the German *Bild* with regional editions.

river. White space running across text, made by spaces between words, which looks unsightly.

RNAB. *See* REGIONAL NEWSPAPER ADVERTISING BUREAU.

road show. A film, video, exhibition or sales presentation taken from town to town, perhaps using a purpose-built vehicle.

roadside poster. As distinct from transport sites. Historically, outdoor advertising is divided into two forms, transportation extending to advertising on and in vehicles, and on premises. Various contractors offer packages of roadside poster campaigns, covering size, number of panels, areas, periods, average weekly OSCAR audience per panel, package cost and comments on special characteristics.

roll-on pilfer-proof cap. Form of security packaging in which the cap of a bottle is freed by ripping off a ring of aluminium on the bottle neck. H. G. Kalish ROPPCAP system.

roll out. Number of names addressed in a mailing, sometimes as decided after a test mailing.

Rollcall. Targeting system which provides access to household counts and demographic penetration analysis for any postally defined area in Great Britain. SUPER PROFILE counts available at postcode sector level. Each household can be defined as 'family', 'single male' or 'single female'. Counts can be automatically aggregated to TV area, county or any other predefined regions. Counts based on current Electoral Roll, not Census. Includes new voters, new occupants, known responders to direct mail. Credit and Data Marketing Services Ltd, Liverpool.

rolling launch. Gradual launch of a new product with stages such as TEST MARKETING, followed by zonal marketing region by region until national market covered.

Roman letters. Upright type as distinct from sloping ITALICS.

Roman numerals. As written I for one, V for five, X for 10, C for 100, D for 500 and M for 1,000.

Rorschach ink blot test. In MOTIVATIONAL RESEARCH, a projective test requiring the respondent to identify shapes which look like ink blots. Developed by Hermann Rorschach, Swiss psychiatrist. Anxieties, inadequacies and conflicts of respondents are revealed by their interpretation of the ink blot shapes.

roseland. Acronym for rest of south-east England outside London.

Rosenzweig picture frustration test. MOTIVATIONAL RESEARCH test consisting of cartoons in which one character is frustrated by another. A balloon has to be completed to show what the respondent imagines the frustrated character would say in the pictured situation. Reveals respondent's attitudes and motives regarding a particular topic which would be the subject of the survey.

Roses Creative Awards. Annual advertising awards sponsored by ADLINE. Categories include TV, radio, trade and consumer press, posters. Gold, silver, bronze trophies. Attracts more than 500 entries from agencies outside London.

rostrum shooting. Not live shooting, but camera work inside studio using camera on adjustable device with subjects such as stills or scale models on adjustable table.

rotary. Printing machine having rotating plate cylinder. Opposite to FLATBED.

rotasign. Illuminated light-box displaying a sequence of up to 40 advertisements on continuous reel. Found in supermarkets and shopping precincts.

rotating sample. A sample in which a panel is used for different periods of a survey, say, quarterly. *See* AGB HOME AUDIT SERVICE.

rotoscope. Method of trying to simulate reality when producing animated (films) cartoons, by tracing directly from live-action film footage.

roundel. Circular LOGOTYPE similar to that of ICI.

ROW. RUN-OF-WEEK.

ROY. RUN-OF-YEAR.

Royal Warrant. Suppliers of goods or services to members of the Royal Family may receive award of Royal Warrant. Coat of arms may be used in advertising or in decorations of premises or vehicles. Holders become members of Royal Warrant Holders Association. Strict rules regarding use of Royal Arms. Usage normally 10 years.

RRP. *See* RECOMMENDED RETAIL PRICE.

rub and reveal panels. Applied to DIRECT MAIL envelopes like SCRATCH CARDS, a latex area that can be rubbed off with a coin to reveal a message. Made by Chapman Envelopes. *See also* COIN RUB, LATEX SILVER SCRATCH OFF.

rule. Thick, thin, wavy, dotted or any other special design of line used in print, as in rule separating a column of text, or outlining a coupon.

run-around. Type surrounding a picture or other shape. Artistic but often detrimental to readability of text. Best avoided in advertisements and sales letters.

run of day/period/week/month spots. TV commercials, usually at cheaper rate, which a station can use at its discretion.

run-of-paper. Advertisement inserted wherever there is space available and charged at ordinary position rate.

run-of-week. In publishing, advertisement inserted at publisher's discretion in one issue of a daily, during a week.

run-of-year. In publishing, advertisement which publisher may insert at his discretion and at lower rate, in any month's issue of a magazine. In TV, low filler rate for commercial shown at discretion of station.

run-on. 1. In printing and publishing, type which is set continuously as in a classified advertisement. 2. Additional copies of a piece of print. 3. Take copy from one page to another, as when extra words are inserted.

running head, headlines. In a book or magazine, repetition of title at top of each page.

running on charge. Price charged by MAILING LIST owner for names not used although available.

S

S4C. Welsh Channel 4. Programmes began November 1, 1982 under Welsh Fourth Channel Authority. There is priority for Welsh language programmes, but some Channel 4 programmes are used, often at different times.

sachets. Small packages usually containing one portion of dose, made of paper, foil or plastic. Used for tea bags, coffee, sugar, insecticides, shampoo, car wax, soup, condiments.

saddle-stitch. Method of binding magazines with wire stitching from spine to centre-spread so that pages lie flat when magazine opened.

safety, safe products. *See* CONSUMER PROTECTION ACT 1987. The BCAP and the IBA Code have sections dealing with safety in advertisements as regards children or young people. Dangerous situations which children might copy should not be shown. *See* CHILDREN AND ADVERTISING, and CHILDREN AND TELEVISION ADVERTISING.

sagacity life cycle groupings. Basic thesis is that people have different aspirations and behaviour patterns as they go through their life cycle. Four main stages of life cycle are defined (dependent, pre-family, family, late) which are sub-divided by income and occupation groups. The occupation groups are divided into white (ABC^1) and blue (C^{2}DE). Research Services Ltd.

Sale of Goods Act 1893. Act implies that contract guarantees a seller has a good title to transfer to customer. Important in DIRECT RESPONSE marketing, in which there are terms and conditions implied in resulting sale. *See* amendments under SUPPLY OF GOODS (IMPLIED TERMS) ACT 1973, UNFAIR CONTRACT TERMS ACT 1977.

sales lead. Good enquiry resulting from advertising which a salesman can follow up. Advertisements must give a reader the opportunity to refuse or invite a representative's call.

sales promotion. Short-term below-the-line activities, usually at POINT OF SALE but can be via media, to launch product or maintain or increase sales. Includes premium offers, flash packs, charity-linked schemes, banded packs, on-pack offers, mail-ins, sampling, in-store promotions, prize contests, etc.

salience. In an opinion survey, the extent to which respondents are interested in or aware of the subject being studied.

Sally Awards. Annual awards for advertising campaigns which were never executed. Sally Awards Ltd, Birmingham.

salutation. Personal greeting at beginning of a letter, which may be personalised by insertion of name by word processor or LASER PRINTING. Dear Sir/Madam should never be used.

same size. Instruction to reproduce artwork the same size as it is.

sample. 1. In SALES PROMOTION, a specimen or free sample. 2. In marketing research, a representative number of people to be questioned in a survey. *See* QUOTA SAMPLE, RANDOM SAMPLE.

sample mailing. Test mailing before conducting a full mailing. A single proposition, or different appeals or offers may be tested to see which produces best response.

sampling error. As used particularly in RANDOM SAMPLING, standard error of a percentage estimate is:

$$s = \frac{p(100 - p)}{n}$$

where p is the percentage estimate and n is the sample size.

sampling frame. Specified make-up of population data on which marketing research sample is to be based. Examples: membership lists, census returns, types of dwellings. Primary sampling area can be chosen areas, secondary sampling frame can be selected people in these areas.

sampling points. Places where interviews are conducted. The more sampling points, the more representative the sample.

sandwich-board advertising. Outdoor advertising medium, person carrying placards on chest and back.

sans serif. A type without lines or serifs at extremities of characters, e.g. Gill Sans, Univers, Helvetica.

satellite. Device placed in space by a rocket and orbiting earth. In television, it permits the relay of live programmes including news events world-wide. Enables newspapers to be transmitted for international publication. Also used for cross-frontier TV programmes such as Sky, received either by individual dish or via cable television. *See* ASTRA, SMITH TELEVISION, W. H. and DIRECT BROADCASTING BY SATELLITE.

satellite TV. In Europe, four main satellites which can be received by dish or cable. ASTRA: various SKY channels and W. H. Smith Television; Eutelsat 1 F1: multi-channel satellite including Sky, Super Channel, French TV; Intelsat VA F11: multi-channel satellite including CNN, Children's Channel, Premiere; BSB—British Satellite Broadcasting, three channels launched 1990, two afterwards.

satirical advertising. Advertising which contains ironical comment on the advertiser, product or service. Kind of wry humour, laughing at itself to make sales point.

saturation advertising. Excessive advertising to make impact on the market. Once used by detergent advertisers on TV, provoking public criticism. Replaced by advertising aimed at achieving a certain percentage coverage of market or a given volume of audience ratings, after which the commercial is withdrawn for a while. Some commercials (e.g. Brooke Bond PG Tips) have been used for up to 18 months because they were never shown for too long a period to bore.

saturation distribution. As occurs with FREE NEWSPAPERS delivered door-to-door, street-by-street throughout circulation area.

scale, law of. Large bold type contrasts with small light type. Dark colours advance, pale colours recede as with red versus pale blue.

scale model. Miniature made to correct scale as with aircraft, trains and ships used for travel agency displays, or models of houses or of a construction project.

scamp. Rough visual or sketch of an advertisement which is not measured exactly like a LAYOUT.

scan mark. Control mark on pre-printed colour WEBS which is read by an electronic scanner to obtain correct register with black and white pages when newspaper is printed.

scanachrome. Way of producing full-colour displays and posters on any flexible material. *See* NECCI ENLARGER.

Scantex 2000. Machine capable of producing complete setting and artwork of an advertisement or other print. Retouches halftones; scans, retouches and enhances tone or line illustrations; reverses black to white, solid or tinted; produces areas of clean, even tints (including vignettes) in percentage and screen ruling required; rotates type; modifies; sets automatic runrounds; produces logos as type; links up with IBM compatible PCs. Sets pin sharp type 1 to 90mm cap height. Combinations of these features can be imposed together and viewed on 17″ interactive graphic monitor and output via Image Setter on film or paper, right or wrong reading, up to a full 20 x 24 image area. Scangraphic Visutek Ltd. Leatherhead.

scatter proofs. Used for checking quality of illustrations in photo-mechanical reproduction, several pictures being proofed together.

SCC. Single column centimetre.

scene advertising. *See* BELOW-THE-LINE ADVERTISING.

Schafline high-definition system. Graphic system in which photographs are retouched to produce a very clear dot screen, line screen or special effect halftones so that halftones reproduce sharply on newsprint. Schafline Ltd, London.

score. Crease or fold, as with board covers.

scotchprint. Proof taken on plastic material from LETTERPRESS plate or form, to convert colour plate from letterpress to offset-litho.

scratch and sniff. Scented printing inks as used for SALES PROMOTION gimmicks.

scratch cards. Sales promotion cards with latex patches which can be scratched off to reveal a lucky number, value of voucher, or fruit machine symbols. *See* COIN RUB, LATEX SILVER SCRATCH OFF.

screamer. Exclamation mark.

screen. Dot formation for reproducing continuous tone pictures by halftone screen. *See* HALFTONE, HALFTONE SCREEN RATINGS.

screen clash. Distortion due to two or more halftone screens (as in colour work) having been positioned at wrong angles, resulting in a blurred dot pattern.

screened line art. Line drawings, screened in either negative or positive form, and possibly including graduated screens; can achieve a softer halftone effect. Screened line art can also be set on screen backgrounds. *See* SCANTEX 2000.

screened type. Laying a screen on type which can produce a ghostly or grey effect. Produced with digital typesetting.

script. Typeface resembling handwriting.

sealed mailer. DIRECT MAIL insert with perforated tear-off strip.

sealing perforation. Mailshot with perforated edges which have to be torn off in order to open the piece.

Sears, Roebuck. One of the pioneers of MAIL ORDER catalogue trading in the USA in mid-19th century.

second colour. Usually a colour additional to black, unless another colour is the main colour.

secondary colour. Product of mixing two primary colours, e.g. blue and yellow to make green.

secondary media. Support media for primary. Choice and relevance of primary and secondary media may be the opposite for different advertisers. Should not therefore be confused with ABOVE-THE-LINE and BELOW-THE-LINE media. A fmcg company might choose press and TV as primary media, exhibitions and POINT OF SALE material as secondary; a DIRECT RESPONSE company might use DIRECT MAIL and catalogues as primary media and press as secondary.

secondary readership. Others who read a publication in addition to the original buyers, e.g. members of family, neighbours, friends, pass-round readership at workplaces, those in waiting and reception rooms, etc.

secondary research, sources. Already published or existing material. Not original primary research.

secondary usage. After-use of a container which may make original purchase more attractive, e.g. sweet jar or tin can have kitchen use.

security packaging. *See* CHILD-RESISTANT CONTAINER, ROLL-ON PILFER-PROOF, TAMPER EVIDENT, TERROR TAMPERING.

See You In Barking. Tracking study into awareness of bus advertising, conducted in 1987 by British Market Research Bureau for London Transport advertising. Some 70 different bus side campaigns were measured. Interviewers questioned some 500 adults at 40 sampling points and during home interviews. Test campaign was run by LTA with poster of barking dogs and a caption 'See You In Barking' placed on 750 T-SIDES between mid-April and mid-May. After 2 weeks, 32% recalled poster, after 4 weeks 37%. Other campaigns achieved from 8% to 63% awareness, but most achieved 32%–37%.

seed. Unique name inserted in MAILING LIST for checking of list usage. Also called sleeper or trap name.

segmentation. Limitation of prospect list to most likely buyers. Way of making most efficient use of DIRECT MAIL list or DATA-BASE.

segmented publication. Small circulation journal aimed at minority or special interest readership.

segments. Divisions of time on British television in which advertisements appear, rates varying according to whether they are peak or off-peak segments. *See* MARKET SEGMENT.

self-completion panel. Research panel in which respondents complete pre-coded diaries and return them to the research company each week, usually recording purchases. For an example *see* AGB MARKET TRACK ATTWOOD SERVICE.

self cover. Cover pages of a brochure or catalogue being of the same paper as inside pages.

self-liquidating offer. SALES PROMOTION premium offer which pays for itself. The applicant sends proof of purchase, such as token or wrapper, plus cash for the bargain offer on which promoter makes neither profit nor loss.

self-mailer. DIRECT MAIL shot which requires no envelope for either despatch or reply.

self-regulatory. Voluntary ethical control, such as BRITISH CODE OF ADVERTISING PRACTICE, which is most effective when it is preventive.

self-seal polythene envelopes. *See* POLYTHENE ENVELOPES.

semantic differential. Way of evaluating attitudes by inviting respondents to express likes and dislikes on a scale ranging from, e.g., excellent to bad which can be calculated $+3$, $+2$, $+1$, -1, -2, -3. Figures can be aggregated. Developed by C. E. Osgood.

semi-display. In classified advertisement section of a newspaper those advertisements in which the copy is not run on but set in a variety of type sizes and displayed.

sentence completion test. In MOTIVATIONAL RESEARCH a projective test requiring the filling in of blanks in sentences or phrases.

separation artwork. Artwork in which separate layers are made for each colour to be printed, using translucent overlays.

sequential launch. Phasing a product launch zone by zone, thus avoiding a national campaign spread too thinly.

serial association. Way of post-testing advertisements by asking members of a DISCUSSION GROUP to associate ideas with it. Result can show what desirable, undesirable, predictable, unexpected responses are provoked by the advertisement being tested.

series. 1. Range of sizes in a certain type face. 2. Set of editorial features or TV programmes. 3. A number of insertions in a journal, for which a series discount is given.

serif. Lines at extremities or stems and arms of letters. A serif type (e.g. Times, Goudy, Plantin) is easier to read in small type sizes, and in text matter, than SANS SERIF type (such as Erbar, Univers or Helvetica). Books and newspapers printed mainly in serif types. Some litho printed sales literature which is printed in sans serif type can be less legible in serif type. When shiny paper is used, the serif type is more legible than sans serif.

serigraphy. SILK SCREEN or screen printing.

set. 1. To typeset. 2. Width of a type character.

set solid. Type set with no leading or space between the lines.

setmeter. Electronic device used for TV audience measurement as part of system to produce BARB figures. Records on heat sensitive paper details of when TV receiver was switched on or off and to which station it is tuned. *See also* PEOPLEMETER.

Sex Discrimination Act 1975. Bans advertisements which indicate an intention to discriminate on grounds of sex. Applies particularly to recruitment advertising, resulting in inoffensive terms such as salesperson. Equal Opportunities Commission has powers of enforcement.

shadow box. *See* VARIOMETER.

Shah, Eddie. Although unsuccessful himself, Shah revolutionised the British newspaper scene by pioneering a break with print unions in 1983 which led to an exodus of nationals from Fleet Street to new plants or contract printers, replacing hot metal foundries with computerised typesetting fed by direct input single keying paperless rooms. Shah launched *Today* in February 1986 as the first British colour-litho daily, but following failure to find right niche in the market sold out to Lonrho June 1986, who subsequently sold paper to News International. Under new editorship sales improved, but the publication was losing £10m a year in 1988. Shah launched *The Post* November 1988, which failed after 33 issues, losing £9m. Sold his free newspaper chain, and concentrated on TV production company. Nevertheless, his impact is remarkable in that it gave lead to new newspaper technologies, bringing colour to newspapers as never before, and breaking uneconomic trade union stranglehold.

shank. Body of a metal type character.

share of audience. Percentage of the total audience to radio that are listening to a particular station.

shareplan, shared distribution. In door-to-door MAIL DROPS, the delivery of more than one item at the same time. Contractors accept non-competing items at special rate. Can be disliked by householders who object to doormat litter.

sheet. Whole piece of paper before folding or cutting.

sheet-fed. Printing from separate sheets of paper, not from a reel or WEB.

shelf edging. As seen on edges of shelves behind shop or bar counter, narrow adhesive strips of paper bearing advertising messages.

shelf-talker. POINT OF SALE display arranged on shopkeeper's shelf to promote product.

Shell scheme. Simple ready-made exhibition stands supplied at a cheap rate by exhibition promoters. Virtually cube-shaped with one end open to aisle and public.

shift research. *See* OPINION POLL.

ship cinemas, TV. Medium for advertising duty free and other goods on sale on cruise ships, ferries and other vessels.

ship exhibitions. Floating exhibitions on ships fitted out for the purpose, which either sail from port to port, or remain in one dock.

shoot. To take a photograph, or take pictures for a film or video.

shooting script. The camera script as distinct from the actor's script for a film or video. Sets out scenes with directions, and may be arranged out of sequence to provide convenient plan of actions, especially regarding on-location shots.

shop audit. *See* DEALER AUDIT.

shopping. Looking for a new advertising agency, as in 'shopping around'.

shopping list test. MOTIVATIONAL RESEARCH projective test, where respondents are asked to describe the character and possible behaviour of a person likely to buy items on given shopping list.

shopping patterns. *See* LUPIN DATABASE.

short rate. Higher rate charged for fewer insertions when advertiser does not take up full volume of advertising for which he had contracted originally.

shot. Single mailing of DIRECT MAIL piece.

show through. Dark areas of print on reverse side showing through a light-toned picture or area of white space, giving dirty effect to an advertisement. Problem with some TABLOIDS which have long print-runs and are printed at high speed on poor quality paper.

showcard. POINT OF SALE piece strutted to stand or pierced to hang, printed on card, metal or plastic. Used for shop window, and shelf displays.

sidehead. Crosshead. Sub-heading between paragraphs of text and ranged left.

sidestitch or stab stitch. Form of wire binding, stitching pages from front to back. Used for thicker magazines when SADDLE-STITCHING unsuitable. Covers are drawn on, giving a flat spine. While pages are less easy to open than with saddle-stitching they do not burst free as with PERFECT BINDING.

signature slogan. Strapline or pay-off slogan at the foot of an advertisement. May repeat a TV jingle. Creates corporate image such as BMW's The Ultimate Driving Machine. *See* BASELINE, STRAPLINE.

signatures. In book binding, sets of 16 or 32 pages gathered for binding. Originates from printer's signature marking sets of pages.

signs. Visual outdoor advertising with a very long history, e.g. inn sign, apothecary's bottles, barber's red and white pole, wheelwright's wheel, and so on up to modern day signs such as those of petrol pumps and lighted signs including NEWS-CASTERS in city centres.

silk screen printing. Serigraphic printing process of Chinese origin which used a mesh of human hair. Stencils are made of the printing design, and ink squeezed through the screen made of silk, nylon, organdie or metal mesh. Much used for printing posters such as window bills, but versatile because many materials and non-flat surfaces can be printed. Can be applied to paper, board, wood, plastics, metal, glass. Used to print dials, book jackets, pens, ties, T-shirts, ashtrays, bottles.

silver market. Those over 60 years of age. *See* PSYCHOGRAPHIC TYPES.

simulcasting. ILR stations broadcasting the same programme on both AM and FM frequencies. *See* SPLIT-FREQUENCY.

single key stroking. *See* DIRECT INPUT. Process of keying in copy in computerised newsrooms and newspaper advertisement offices where there is no foundry and no hot-metal typesetting.

site. Poster location.

site classification. Grading of sites, with different rentals, according to location and, as in the case of London Underground, traffic volume.

size up. Instruction to printer to set type a size larger, when proof reading.

skip instructions. In a marketing research questionnaire some questions may not be relevant to certain respondents, and the interviewer is instructed to move on to the next relevant question.

Sky Channel. Founded October 1981 as Satellite Television Plc with aim of delivering a European commercial TV service by low-powered satellite. Began transmitting on 26 April 1982, two hours nightly in English to cable nets in Norway and Finland, plus TV homes in Malta, using Orbital Test Satellite (OTS-2). Switzerland added in July 1982. In June 1983 News International Plc (Rupert Murdoch, chairman) acquired 65% of Satellite TV's capital. He leased a channel from British Telecom on the European Communications Satellite (ECS-1), administered by EUTELSAT and introduced the first daily European pop music shows with *Cable Countdown*. The new name Sky Channel was adopted in January 1984, and by now it could be received by cable homes in the UK, West Germany, Austria, followed by The Netherlands and Sweden. In 1985 Sky celebrated its 3rd million household to be connected to its network. *Pop Formulae* was introduced weekly in 1986, co-produced with the Dutch *Tros*. In the UK, Sky production took on bigger studios for its *Trax Fun Factory*, *Movietime* and *Deadly Ernest Horror Shows*. Many new programmes were created. In 1987, Sky produced the live *World Music Video Awards*, with a global TV link-up for this three-hour event. The first PETAR survey ranked Sky as the leading pan-European satellite TV station. By 1988 Sky reached 11.4m homes in 19 countries with a potential of 29.6m viewers. The ASTRA satellite was launched from French Guinea in December 1988, and in February 1989, based on Luxembourg, Sky Channel directed programmes at UK for reception by household dishes or by cable TV. Initially a shortage of dishes made reception meagre, with the controversy over BSB's claim to better quality, and the problem of a ban on homes having two dishes to receive each. Cable companies exploited their ability to deliver Sky Channel programmes without the need for a dish. Sky Channel began in 1989 with Sky News, Eurosport, Sky Movies and 24-hour Sky News, and followed with more programmes later. Listings are published in Murdoch newspapers, *The Sun*, *The Times*, *News of the World* and *Sunday Times*.

slab serif. Kind of typeface with serifs of the same thickness as stems and arms of characters. Egyptian typefaces, e.g. Cairo, Karnak, Rockwell. Useful as display faces, but also legible as text type. Used for ITT logo.

slash. The oblique stroke (/).

sleeper. *See* SEED.

sleeper effect. Occurs in opinion poll research when respondents show a delayed shift of opinion after exposure to a message.

sleeve. In photogravure printing, cylindrical printing plate with recessed image. Cells of varying depths hold ink according to the required tonal effect. Surface has grid which is scraped by a doctor's blade to remove excess ink. *See* PHOTOGRAVURE, KLISCHOGRAPH HARD-DOT GRAVURE.

slip edition. Local edition of a newspaper with an extra page containing local or regional news slipped in.

slipping. Pasting an amendment on a poster.

slogan. Rather like a TV JINGLE, a catchy phrase which helps people to remember a product. Some persist long after original use, like 'Guinness is Good For You', or continue to be used for decades like 'Ah, Bisto!' *See also* STRAPLINE, SIGNATURE SLOGAN which also establish a CORPORATE IMAGE.

slot. Commercial break in TV programme.

small ads. Smalls or CLASSIFIED ADVERTISEMENTS.

SMATV. Satellite Master Antenna Television.

Smith Television, W. H. Satellite TV company using two transponders on the ASTRA satellite which is also used by SKY CHANNEL. The company has an agreement with the German Bundespost to broadcast Sportkanal, a German version of its Screensport, throughout Federal Republic. WHSTV also broadcasts via Intelsat 5 satellite and received by cable subscribers in UK and some other European countries. WHSTV broadcasts *Lifestyle* and interactive *The Cable Jukebox*, plus *Kindernet*, children's programme for Dutch cable.

snipe. Overlay or strip of copy added to poster. *See* SLIPPING.

soap opera commercials. Series of TV commercials with characters who continue a story from one commercial to another like the *Dallas*, *Dynasty*, *EastEnders* soap operas. Examples: Cointreau, Nescafé Gold Blend, Renault 25, Heinz, Oxo, British Telecom.

soaps. Originating from American radio serials sponsored by soap companies, now applied to popular TV series such as *Coronation Street*, *Brookside*, *Dallas*, *Dynasty*, *EastEnders*, *Emmerdale Farm* and *Neighbours*.

social grades. Replacing socio-economic groups (based on income), social grades (based on employment) are used for JICNARS National Readership Survey and other marketing research surveys. A (Upper middle class) 3%; B (Middle class) 13%; C^1 (Lower middle class—white collar) 22%; C^2 (Skilled working class—blue collar) 32%; D (Semi-skilled, unskilled working class) 20%; and E (Lowest level of subsistence) 9%. Can be related to national dailies: A *The Times*, *Financial Times*; B *Daily Telegraph*, *The Independent*, *The Guardian*; C^1 *Daily Express*, *Daily Mail*, *Today*; C^2, D, E, *The Sun*, *Daily Mirror*, *Daily Star*.

soft focus. Special photographic effect which is not sharp.

solid. Type is set solid when there is no leading or white space between lines.

solus. 1. An advertisement which stands alone on the page. 2. A solus poster site (e.g. a BULLETIN BOARD or SUPERSITE). 3. An exhibition stand which occupies an ISLAND SITE, and has all four sides open to aisles and visitors.

solus distribution. In door-to-door delivery, a single MAIL DROP. May be targeted to a defined geographical area such as by use of ACORN. *See* SHAREPLAN, SHARED DISTRIBUTION.

solus spots. TV commercials unaccompanied by other commercials.

sortation. DATABASE system used for DIRECT MAIL which allows stored information to be selected according to specified characteristics, e.g. name, within date, media code, region. Also, as in the sortation plan of the MAILSORT system of sorting direct mail shots on the basis of 1,520 direct selections of postcodes whereby mail goes direct to delivery offices, and 80 are residue selections to post offices where mail is sorted to delivery offices.

sound recording. According to the COPYRIGHT, DESIGNS AND PATENTS ACT 1988 a sound recording means—(a) a recording of sounds, from which the sounds may be reproduced, or (b) a recording of the whole or any part of a literary, dramatic or musical work, from which sounds reproducing the work or part may be produced, regardless of the medium on which the recording is made or the method by which the sounds are reproduced; and film means a recording on any medium from which a moving image may by any means be produced.

Sp. In typesetting, spacing between type characters.

space buyer. Person in an advertising agency who buys advertisement media. Media buyer.

special or preferred position. Advertisement position in a publication which is rated higher because of its special or higher readership.

spectaculars. Very large poster sites such as those erected above escalator shafts in London Underground.

spectrum. Full range of colours from violet to red.

speech bubble. As used in cartoons or with other pictures, spoken words written in balloons.

speed premium. In DIRECT RESPONSE marketing, an incentive to spur action such as the offer of a gift or discount if the order sent within, e.g., seven days.

spelunking. In DIRECT RESPONSE marketing, targeting a campaign at specific prospects such as those interested in certain products. *See* FISHING, MINING.

spend. The advertising budget or APPROPRIATION.

spine. Backbone or back edge of a book.

split-frequency. ILR stations can broadcast on both AM and FM frequencies, the latter being most popular, but if separate programmes are broadcast on each frequency this becomes split-frequency (virtually two radio stations) and different programmes can attract different advertisers. The original station can appeal to the core radio audience (15–24yr olds) and additional station (or frequency) can appeal to older audience e.g. Capital's 'Gold', with 'classic' pop music, aims at 30–45yr olds. Can also provide separate programmes for ethnic audiences.

split run test. *See* A/B SPLIT METHOD.

split transmissions. TV transmissions from different transmitters which permit advertisers to test alternative commercials. Offered by Yorkshire Television and HTV. *See* STATS SCAN.

sponsored radio. As offered by PPM Radio Waves, networked sponsored radio shows such as Midland Bank 'Rockline' phone-in programme, Pepsi Cola 'Countdown Show', Budweiser 'Motown Story', and Nat West 'Live Action Concert'. Also, sponsorship of information announcements by radio presenters, called barter/syndication and special sponsorships such as travel, financial reports and Continental Airlines' sponsorship of Capital's Flying Eye aeroplane which monitors London's traffic.

sponsorship. Financial support by commercial organisations for arts, books, sports, events, expeditions, education and so on. May be for advertising, marketing or public relations purposes, or combination of these. Often dependent on subject being televised, but independent of TV programmes and not to be confused with sponsorship of whole programmes which is common in some parts of the world. However, in 1989 mild form of sponsorship or 'funding' of certain classes of programme introduced, e.g. 'sponsoring' of ITV weather reports by Powergen and concerts by British Gas on BBC TV. *See also* SPONSORED RADIO.

spot. Single showing of TV commercial. *See* FILLER SPOTS, FIXED SPOTS.

spot colour. Use in press advertisement of a single second colour for, say, brand name or LOGOTYPE.

spot rate. Rate for single TV commercial as distinct from packages.

spread. A double-page spread, i.e. a pair of facing pages.

spread pasting dates. Spacing out of dates for pasting of posters so that they appear at stated intervals.

spread traffic. Form of media readership research to measure the proportion of readers of an issue who read or looked at each spread in a magazine, producing a score for an average spread.

SRA sizes. For offset printing machines, SRA paper sizes are slightly over similar A sizes to allow for bleed or to allow trimming of grip edges. *See* PAPER SIZES.

s/s. *See* SAME SIZE.

stand-out test. Method of researching the ability of a pack to stand out from existing competitors. The new pack is photographed among others on a shelf. Respondents are then shown picture on a screen and invited to identify the pack being tested. The time taken to find pack is then measured to show how quickly or slowly it is spotted.

standard regions. *See* REGISTRAR GENERAL'S STANDARD REGIONS.

standby space. Low cost advertisement space filled at publisher's discretion.

Stats Scan. TV advertising testing service using split transmission on HTV. Electronically monitors the effect of TV advertising on consumer brand purchasing behaviour. Uses two 1,000-strong household panels which are demographically matched and live in the same part of South Wales. One views HTV West and Channel 4, the other HTV Wales and S4C. Launched April 1989. Organised by Nielsen. *See* MATCHED PANELS. Tests can include: copy testing, weights tests, BURST versus DRIP, mixed media schedule evaluation, target group buying evaluation, day-part frequency.

stem. Upright stroke in a type character.

stereotype photographs. Use of stock pictures of different types of people in group depth interviewing. The respondents are asked which products they think would be bought by each person pictured.

sterling value. In marketing research, monetary value placed on total market for a product.

stock. Quality or type of paper or film to be used, e.g. 35mm stock.

stock footage. Film footage which may be hired for use in films, videos, commercials, either archival or old movie. *See also* LIBRARY SHOT.

stop motion. Technique often used in TV commercials such as packs which unwrap themselves, move independently, faces that come to life on packs, and other 'trick' effects.

store audit. DEALER, shop or retail audit of goods in and sales out.

storyboard. Visual of a TV commercial expressed in cartoon form, each sequence drawn in a shape like a TV screen.

strapline. *see* BASELINE.

strategic research. Research aimed at defining what a new advertising campaign should say.

stratification sample. Means of reducing the size of a national sample or number of SAMPLING POINTS, as in a large RANDOM SAMPLE. The population is divided into parts or strata. It can also mean the division of a sample according to proportion of men and women indicated by census.

streamer. Banner headline spreading across the page.

strip. TV/radio commercial broadcast at the same time on successive days. In press advertising, advertisement of shallow depth extending across all columns at the foot of a page.

stripteaser mailer/insert. DIRECT RESPONSE marketing gimmick, usually sealed, and appealing to the curiosity to discover the message.

structural packaging. Product containers designed to be practical and to distinguish product, e.g. many bottles such as Perrier, Marmite, Mateus Rosé and many convenience packs of individual design.

structured interview. One in which a questionnaire containing pre-determined questions is used.

structured questionnaire. One which has a set of pre-determined questions as distinct from a series of questions posed by an interviewer as in a DEPTH INTERVIEW.

stuffers. Leaflets and instructions placed in packages, e.g. with camera films.

stylebook. Manual of instructions and samples for the presentation of a CORPORATE IDENTITY scheme, e.g. house colour, typography, logo, decoration of vehicles.

subliminal advertising. TV or cinema commercials containing too few frames for the eye to record but sufficient for the mind to capture the message. Banned by IBA Code of Standards and Practice.

sugging. Selling under the guise of research and actively opposed by MARKET RESEARCH SOCIETY. Occurs mostly in telephone selling, but also in pseudo street and doorstep interviews which begin like a survey and lead up to a sales pitch. MRS operates 'checkline' freefone service whereby subscribers can check whether telephone surveys are genuine.

SUGS. Subscription User Group Service. *See* ORACLE.

summative research. Research which records the results of a completed advertising campaign.

Super Profiles. Targeting system which links consumer lifestyle with postal geography, using household counts rather than population estimates. Uses 10 lifestyles ranging from affluent minority to underprivileged, and breaks these down into 36 target markets plus a 37th unclassified. Lifestyle groups are further divided into geodemographic groups such as region, family, occupation, property and car ownership. There are also clusters, 150 neighbourhood groups identified in fine detail. A Super Profile Directory is supplied. Credit and Data Marketing Services Ltd, Liverpool.

Super Search. *See* PROBABILITY RANKING.

supercalendered. Paper which has been polished by hot and cold cylinders or calenders on paper-making machine. Used for popular magazines. *See* GLOSSY.

superior. Small number set above the text to indicate a source reference given at end of article, chapter or book.

supers. Words superimposed on TV commercials.

supersites. 96-sheet size solus outdoor advertising sites. More O'Ferrall offer a supersite package of 165 sites, 40% being in London, with OSCAR score of 137,000 impacts per week per site. *See* BULLETIN BOARD.

Supertype headline fonts. Special digital typesetting headline faces which have four letters with integrated accents instead of basic mathematical signs. Supertype fonts make it unnecessary to use the same drawing for both text and headline setting. Permit compressed headline settings. Scangraphic, Leatherhead, Surrey.

Supply of Goods and Services Act, The, 1982. Two parts: 1. Gives to those who hire items, buy them in part exchange, or have them supplied with a service the same protection enjoyed by other shoppers. 2. Chief part, specifies basic rights which consumers have under Common Law when they receive a service. Work must be performed with reasonable care and skill, and unless otherwise arranged within reasonable time and at reasonable cost.

Supply of Goods (Implied Terms) Act 1973. Amendment of the SALE OF GOODS ACT 1893, guaranteeing consumers' rights under the original Act, and opposing guarantees which claim to exclude such rights. *See also* UNFAIR CONTRACT TERMS ACT 1977.

support media. SECONDARY MEDIA. *See also* PRIMARY MEDIA.

swap mailing. *See* PIGGYBACKING.

swash letter. Ornamental type character.

symbol. An abstract design which identifies an organisation such as those of British Rail, Plessey, Dunlop, British Oxygen, which should be referred to as symbols, not LOGOTYPES.

systematic error. In marketing research, an error caused by bias.

Szondi test. In MOTIVATIONAL RESEARCH the use of a set of cards bearing faces of different characters. The subject is asked to choose one he would most like to sit next to, and one he would prefer not to, not knowing that all the characters are disordered. The purpose of the test is to detect whether respondent will choose character most similar to himself. This can reveal his possible personality change in certain circumstances.

T

tabloid. Small page newspaper such as *Daily Mail*, *Daily Express*, *Today*, *Daily Mirror*, *The Sun*, *Daily Star* compared with large page broadsheets such as *The Times*, *Financial Times*, *Daily Telegraph*, *Independent* and *The Guardian*. Although often used in derogatory sense to describe popular press, the term has been used to describe small format newspapers since 1903. Derived from Henry Wellcome's combination of 'tablet' and 'alkaloid' for his medicinal product in 1884.

Tachistoscope. In research, instrument which makes visual presentations of subjects for very short spells so that respondents only have time to glance at them.

tactical advertising. *See* SALES PROMOTION, SCENE ADVERTISING.

tail. Bottom margin of a page.

take-one cards. Cards attached to posters and taken by passers-by.

tamper-evident, resistant packages. Packages which deter tampering and give security to drug, drink or food contents. Include heatseal banding of bottle necks, press and twist caps, tear-off strips on plastic or metal screw caps. *See* ROLL-ON PILFER-PROOF CAPS, SECURITY PACKAGING, TERROR TAMPERING.

target audience. Audience to which advertising is directed. May be determined by sex, age, SOCIAL GRADE, special interest, geographical location. *See* PSYCHOGRAPHIC TYPES.

Target Group Index. Source of market data owned by BMRB. Based on questionnaires answered by 24,000 adults a year, covering 400 product fields, their demographic characteristics and media exposure.

target sum method. Also called cost of exposure, task approach or objective method of arriving at the advertising appropriation. Once the market objective is decided the cost of advertising to achieve target is estimated.

targeting. Aiming advertising at specific audience and selecting media which do so most effectively and economically. In direct mail and door-to-door distribution, geodemographic systems such as ACORN, MOSAIC, PIN and SUPER PROFILES can be used to select neighbourhoods containing required target market characteristics.

task method. Variation on TARGET SUM METHOD of assessing advertising APPROPRIATION, the budget being planned for particular purposes or campaigns such as a new product launch.

TAT. *See* THEMATIC APPERCEPTION TEST.

taxi-cab advertising. Advertisements in the passenger section, either fixed to panel facing passengers or on underparts of tip-up seats. Also on exterior panel fitted to nearside cab driver's panel.

Taylor Nelson Media. With Taylor Nelson Medical, conducts readership studies among doctors and medical staff; with Taylor Nelson Financial, researches financial magazine readership; with Taylor Nelson Agriculture, evaluates editorial items in farming magazines; with Taylor Nelson Food & Drink, has specialist knowledge of trade press. Techniques used include editorial panels, OMNIBUS QUESTIONNAIRE, telephone interviewing, diary studies (TV), large scale *ad hoc* quantitative surveys, small sample/specialist sample *ad hoc* QUANTITATIVE surveys, and qualitative surveys—using own executives and specialist consultants. Also conducts Comtest press advertisement testing service. Taylor Nelson & Associates, Epsom, Surrey.

TC. *See* TILL CANCELLED.

TCA. *See* TELEVISION CONSUMER AUDIT.

TEA. Terminal education age. (As used in media studies.)

tear sheet. Serving as a file or voucher copy of an advertisement, specimen page or advertisement torn from a publication.

teletext. Alphanumeric TV information systems which viewers with appropriate sets can receive off-air. Examples are Ceefax (BBC) and ORACLE (ITV), the latter also carrying advertisements.

television. Became an advertising medium in Britain following the Television Act 1955. Has merits of a multi-million audience, vision, sound, movement and colour. British ITV system sells time to advertisers whose commercials appear in natural breaks in programmes provided by contractors such as Thames, London Weekend, regional companies, Channel 4 and TV-am. *See* INDEPENDENT TELEVISION.

Television Consumer Audit, The. Conducted by AGB Market Information, copyright jointly owned by AGB, Central Television, Granada Television, London Weekend Television, TVS, Thames Television, Tyne Tees Television and Yorkshire Television. Uses a continuous panel of 6,300 homes representative of Great Britain. Ulster panel of 400 homes. Each home is visited weekly by an AGB interviewer who records purchases of meat and frozen foods. (Packs are retained until interviewer has recorded them.) The results are grossed up to represent total population. Monitors trends in market structure by brand, retailer, trade sector, price brand, product sector, pack size etc. Reports 2 weeks after period end.

television producer. Advertising agency executive who plans TV commercials for clients, selecting outside director and production company.

television rating. TVR. Way of measuring exposure/impacts of individual TV spots according to recorded audience figure for programme in which the spot appears. A TV campaign can aim to achieve a certain volume of TVRs, after which it may be withdrawn.

Television Register, The. Monitors TV/radio commercials for

TELEVISION RESPONSE HANDLING

advertisers/agencies. Part of Advertising Research Services group which includes the MEDIA REGISTER.

television response handling. As with holiday advertising, TV programme companies accept enquiries produced by commercials and supply names and addresses to advertisers. They also accept orders phoned in to a computer service which supplies advertisers with print-outs of orders within 24 hours. Has been used by record companies.

template. Shape or sheet with cut-outs used as drawing aid, or for printing solid panels, perhaps of a second colour on which text is printed in black.

terror tampering. Insertion of poison or other dangerous substances in packages, usually in shops, by terrorists and demonstrators, resulting in the design of deterrent packages. *See* TAMPER-EVIDENT, RESISTANT PACKAGES, SECURITY PACKAGING.

test area or town. Area used in TEST-MARKETING which is representative of the broadscale market, having similar customers, shops and media such as regional TV.

test input. Simulation of an advertisement or commercial, for pre-testing purposes, but at minimum cost.

test marketing. Means of testing a product and the marketing strategy in a miniature market situation. The object is often to see whether a given percentage of the market can be achieved. *See* TEST AREA OR TOWN. Not to be confused with PRODUCT PRE-TESTING. Test marketing the final insurance before going national. Nevertheless, some 50% of products which enjoy successful test marketing fail to sell nationally. There are usually three stages: pre-test stage when market is nil, to establish base; actual test to measure initial and repeat sales; and post-test to consolidate results.

testimonial. Defined by BCAP as any reference made by an advertiser to the favourable opinion of another in circumstances in which the consumer is likely to give added credence to that opinion because of the ostensible independence of the person or institution said to hold it. Users often offer surprising testimonials. Some testimonials are by users, others are endorsements by celebrities who are paid a fee. In the history of advertising the most famous testimonials are probably those of the society ladies who delighted in allowing their portraits to appear in Pond's face cream, advertisements (originating in Ireland) with the statement 'I always use Pond's'. BCAP Part B, 10.6, says that when fictitious characters in an advertisement express satisfaction with the advertiser's product, care should be taken to avoid consumers confusing them (or their ostensible experiences) with real people or their experiences.

text. The body of undisplayed copy forming the reading matter. *See* TEXT TYPE.

text mark. In print instructions or corrections, mark made within the text itself (e.g. underlining word to be set in italics) in addition to marks made in the margin.

text type. Type used for setting body matter, usually smaller than 12pt, and preferably serifed for easy reading, such as Times, Plantin, Garamond.

TGI. *See* TARGET GROUP INDEX.

thematic apperception test. Projective test used in MOTIVATIONAL RESEARCH. The respondent is shown a set of pictures, such as press cuttings or advertisements, and asked to invent a story about each one in turn. Some of the pictures could feature in advertising. The test reveals what respondent reads into pictures, his reactions and his personality. *See also* PSYCHODRAWING.

themed break. In TV advertising, two or more spots booked to appear in same break for different products made by the same advertiser.

thermography. Printing process that produces a raised surface resembling DIE-STAMPING, as often used for letterheads. Printed sheets are dusted with resinous powder which, under heat, fuses with ink, swells and gives print a raised, glazed appearance.

third class mail. Direct mailshots that benefit from Post Office rebate schemes and may not be treated as urgently as first or even second class mail.

third-party mailing. *See* PIGGYBACKING.

third wave agencies. New generation of small creative agencies, succeeding those A LA CARTE AGENCIES which have become larger ones. Claim to give better service because of closer relationship with clients.

Third Wave, The. Alvin Toffler's futuristic book about post-industrial society in which he discusses DE-MASSIFICATION of the media. Pan Books, London, 1981. *See* TOFFLER, ALVIN.

threshold effects. Stage in advertising expenditure when advertising proves effective in producing desired results.

thrift packs. Packs with simple design features making them economical to produce, and making price reductions possible.

through-the-line agency. Advertising agency which provides strategic planning service, combining ABOVE-THE-LINE and BELOW-THE-LINE media on a one-stop shopping basis. Such agencies existed in the 1960s until specialist agencies took over. Re-emerged in the late 1980s. *See* UNIQUE COMMUNICATIONS PROPOSITION.

tie-breaker. Method used in prize competitions to reduce the number of winners and unsatisfactory division of the prize. In addition to the main contest a supplementary contest is included such as making a statement on why the competitor always buys the product.

ticketboard. PASTEBOARD.

till cancelled. Outdoor advertising instruction to show posters, or keep a site, until due notice of cancellation given.

time segment. *See* SEGMENTS.

time-shift broadcasts. Phenomenon of VCRs whereby programmes are videotaped and watched at a later time, to the exclusion of programmes then being broadcast. Assessed by BARB.

tip-in. Loose single tip sheet inserted in a newspaper between folded pages, or a single sheet of two pages gummed and not bound into a magazine or book.

tip-on. A detachable item glued to an advertisement or direct mail shot.

TISPC. INSTITUTE OF SALES PROMOTION CONSULTANCIES, THE.

title corner. Advertisement space on either side of the title or masthead of a newspaper. Pairs are called ears.

TNT Mailfast. International private mail service which flies mail to strategic points world-wide for local delivery. Cheaper than ordinary postal rates. Useful for export direct mail. *See also* INTERNATIONAL REPLY SERVICE.

Toffler, Alvin. American author of futuristic books *Future Shock*, THIRD WAVE, THE and *Previews and Premises*, in which he describes post-industrial world of social turmoil and its new life-styles, work roles and the DE-MASSIFICATION of the media.

tone step reproduction. With digital design, a generation of graphic variations to a single stored picture. Halftones can be displayed in numerous grey steps, all of which can be assessed and changed. Various background effects can be created for monochrome, real colours or process colour printing. *See* SCANTEX 2000.

Total Audience Package. Package of commercial radio airtime.

total effective exposure. Measure of reader, viewer or listener exposure to an advertisement or a medium.

total hours. In commercial radio research, total length of time listened to radio, or to a station, by the population group being measured, calculated by summing every 15 minutes listened. *See* SHARE OF AUDIENCE.

Town and Country Planning General Development Order 1977. Contains a clause requiring planning permission for installation, alteration or replacement of a satellite antenna if property is already fitted with one.

TRAC. *See* TUBE RESEARCH AUDIENCE CLASSIFICATION.

tracking study. An intensive and continuous post-advertising study, which goes beyond NEXT DAY RECALL studies, and monitors advertising performance and effects. *See* NIELSEN SCANTRACK for a slightly different meaning.

trade advertising. Advertising aimed at distributors to encourage them to stock goods, using trade press, direct mail and exhibitions.

trade characters. Two types. 1. Characters used to personalise and characterise products. They may be ones specially to do with the product, e.g. Bisto Kids, Johnnie Walker or the Michelin Man; animals associated with the product, e.g. British Industrial Sand camel, White Horse Whisky horse, Black & White Whisky Scottish terriers, or Dulux sheep dog; or licensed characters from, say, cartoons, e.g. Nationwide Anglia Building Society Snoopy, Royal Bank of Scotland Top Cat, or Team Cereal Flintstones. 2. Live characters, as when an advertiser is represented by a costumed character, e.g. Dutch cheese girl.

Trade Descriptions Act 1968. Covers any indication, direct or indirect, given by any means whatsoever with respect to goods or parts of goods. Also insists that in shop sales goods offered at reduced prices must have been available for 28 consecutive days during the previous six months at the higher price on ticket. The Act concerns all advertised claims about quality, method of manufacture, composition, fitness for purpose, tests carried out, place of manufacture, manufacturer, and other history.

trade mark. Any distinctive, registrable brand, heading, label, ticket, name, word or other device, according to the

Trade Marks Act 1936. Extended from products to services by Amendment October 1986. Service mark status is available to service industries.

trade mark, fraudulent use of. Section 300 of the COPY-RIGHT, DESIGNS AND PATENTS ACT 1988 repeats sections 58A–D of the Trade Marks Act 1938, e.g. 58A-1(a) It is an offence ... to apply a mark identical to or nearly resembling a registered trade mark to goods, or to material used or intended to be used for labelling, packaging or advertising goods.

trade name. A name for a product as distinct from a registered trade mark or name, e.g. instant coffee or aspirin. *See* GENERIC BRANDS, REGISTERED TRADE NAMES.

trade propaganda. Misuse of terminology, but sometimes used to describe TRADE ADVERTISING, which is not PROPAGANDA.

trading stamps. Stamps given with purchases, redeemable for gifts. Many schemes run during past 10 years. Green Shield and Pink stamps were very popular in the 1960s and 1970s until supermarkets withdrew support. Co-op stamps were given at petrol stations at one time. Green Shield stamps returned for a time at Mobil Garages. AIR MILES (followed by Virgin's Super Airmiles) launched late 1988.

traditional media. Media advertising, or the above-the-line media of press, TV, radio, cinema and outdoor.

traffic department. Responsible for distribution of instructions and progress chasing in advertising agency.

trailers. For exhibition purposes, trailers from 8ft to 22ft can be bought or hired. Larger ones have roll-out, wind-out and plant-on awnings with matching side curtains, fronts and skirts. Large trailers can also include hospitality units. A typical seller/hirer is Lynton Commercial Units Ltd, Gorton, Manchester, or suppliers of special purpose mobiles such as Club Car (SPM) Ltd, Wellingborough, Northants.

train exhibitions. Exhibitions mounted on special trains and toured to stations, placed in bay or siding, and attended by invited guests.

trannie. Colour transparency.

transfer type. *See* DRY TRANSFER LETTERING.

transient medium. Fleeting advertising medium in which a message cannot be retained (except by taping) such as radio, cinema, TV, loudspeaker van, telecaster, as distinct from press or direct mail advertising.

transmission. Broadcasting of TV programme or commercial.

transparency. Trannie. Full-colour photographic positive on transparent film.

transportation advertising. Although sometimes included with outdoor advertising, can be regarded as a separate medium as the public is often in closer contact and able to absorb longer messages than is possible with, for instance, street posters and signs. Includes all advertising inside and outside public service vehicles and premises and on transportation property.

transpose. Marked on proof as 'trs' meaning change position of setting, as when letters are set in wrong sequence.

trap name. *See* SEED.

treatment. A written description of proposals for making a film or video. When this has been approved or amended, the SHOOTING SCRIPT is created.

Trends. Report on DIRECT RESPONSE campaigns produced by Nationwide Market Research for PRECISION MARKETING and supplied as an insert in that magazine. Reports on advertisers, brands, media, including non-couponed page space, couponed page space, inserts, use of colour, and special aspects such as back-to-back coupons, and coupon details such as keying, telephone ordering facility, premium incentives and whether payment requested with order. Full report published in the

DIRECT RESPONSE ADVERTISING YEARBOOK. Nationwide Market Research Ltd, Basingstoke, Hants.

triadic test. Research test to distinguish the odd one out when respondent is presented with three objects.

trimmed size. Final size print job when sheets have been trimmed. The amount that has to be cut off is called 'trim'.

tripartite. Three-sided representation as occurs with media research committees (e.g. JICNARS) when advertisers, advertising agency and media owners organisations are represented.

triple spotting. Broadcasting of three TV commercials in succession or back to back.

trolley ads. Advertisements on trolleys in supermarkets.

TSA. Total survey area, as used in commercial radio research.

T-side. Advertising space in shape of T on double decker bus sides.

Tube Research Audience Classification. London Underground campaign planner database weighted by latest TGI data, by age, sex, socio-economic groups and frequency of travel on the Underground. Analyses an audience of four million adults. TRAC research conducted by Marplan who recruited 10,000 travellers over 200 stations. Each was given a 28-day diary and detailed lifestyle questionnaire. Nearly 5,000 diaries covering 150,000 journeys were returned. TRAC-PACS, based on research statistics, make it possible to plan individual campaigns with an audience profile that mirrors that of the total Underground audience. There are TRAC-PACS for 48 sheets, 16 sheets and Tube Car Panels. Each TRAC-PAC gives an audience breakdown for, say, 50 48 sheets, 150 16 sheets, 300 16 sheets, 4,000 Tube car panels, 8,000 car panels and other combinations with named stations or lines.

Tube car panels. 8,000 available in London Underground trains. Audience of 3.9 million adults per month, with strong bias towards ABC[1]s and under 35s. Average journey time seven minutes. London Transport Advertising recommend paper makes and qualities. *See* REAR-ILLUMINATED. To avoid fire hazard, car cards must not be laminated. *See* LAMINATE.

tuckboxes. Cardboard containers, bearing customer's name, logo or advertisement, for custom PLAYING CARDS.

TV-am. One of two commercial breakfast TV stations, launched in February 1983. Programmes 6.00am–9.15am. *See* BREAKFAST TV.

TV Homes. Those having a TV set which receives transmissions of acceptable quality from any one or combination of BBC1, BBC2 and ITV.

TVR. *See* TELEVISION RATING.

twenty-eight day clause. *See* TRADE DESCRIPTIONS ACT, 1968.

two-stage sell. In DIRECT RESPONSE marketing, two-stage mailing campaign, first seeking enquiry, and second converting enquiry into sale. Can also apply to OFF-THE-PAGE offers.

two-step gift leads. Offer of a modest gift if a recipient of DIRECT RESPONSE offer takes first step, but offer of a superior gift if second step is taken. First step might be application for catalogue, second step could be making purchase from it.

type area. The printed area of a page surrounded by margins, or that part of an advertisement layout devoted to text.

type family. All varieties of a typeface, e.g. roman, italics, light, medium, bold, extra bold, condensed, expanded.

type-high. In relief printing (LETTERPRESS) common height of all printing metal such as type, rules, line and halftone blocks, this being 0.918 of an inch.

type mark-up. Copy ready for printer with instructions given regarding typefaces and type sizes.

type modification. In digital typesetting, ability to condense or expand type widths.

type series. All sizes in one typeface.

typeface. A design of type such as Goudy, Helvetica, Rockwell, Plantin or Times.

typesetter. Person who sets type. Originally the hand compositor, then the operator of a typesetting machine, and now the keyboard operator of a computerised typesetting machine.

typographer. Person who selects type and instructs typesetter regarding typefaces, typesizes, and measure of type areas or column widths. Produces TYPE MARK-UP.

typographic errors. Literals made by typesetter. With computerised typesetting these errors can be different from those produced with metal typesetting. Word breaks can occur badly because of justification of lines; a key may be pressed for italics and not released correctly so that unintended italics are set. Mostly occurs with litho printing. Proof reading has to be extra vigilant to spot such typographical errors.

typography. Art of selecting typefaces, and of marking up copy for typesetting.

typologies. *See* PSYCHOGRAPHIC TYPES.

U

UCP. *See* UNIQUE COMMUNICATIONS PROPOSITION.

UK Press Gazette. Weekly for journalists which publishes news on publishing world. Quarterly feature on registered trade names. London. 1965.

unaided recall. In marketing research, asking questions without identifying what is being researched. *See* AIDED RECALL.

Underground advertising. *See* ADVERTISING AWARENESS RESEARCH, TRAC, TUBE CAR PANELS.

Unfair Contract Terms Act 1977. Law which makes void those terms of agreement which attempt to exclude obligations regarding title under the SALE OF GOODS ACT 1893.

ungathered. Loose printed sheets not collated in numbered page order.

uni-poles. Tubular-shaped poster sites on pavements or in shopping precincts.

Unique Communications Proposition. Central concept of strategic THROUGH-THE-LINE planning as applied by creative marketing agency Koan of London.

unique selling proposition. Concept introduced by REEVES, ROSSER of New York advertising agency Ted Bates, in 1940s. The identification or, if necessary, creation of a product's exclusive benefit, which forms the advertising theme.

unity, law of. Blending the elements of a design, such as an advertisement layout, to form a unified whole. A unified advertisement thus seen as a whole, and not as a number of individual and perhaps distracting bits.

universe. In marketing research, the population, or those people relevant to the enquiry, from which a RANDOM or QUOTA SAMPLE is taken.

unjustified. Typesetting with a free or ragged right-hand edge. May suit simulation of readers' letters, or for small areas of copy. Tiresome and difficult to read if applied to long runs of copy. Generally best avoided if legibility is to be maximised.

unscrambling. Changing electronic signal into picture and sound, as with satellite TV.

unshift. Keyboard name for lower case type, i.e. small characters.

Unsolicited Goods and Services Acts, 1971, 1975. Cover rights and duties of receivers of unsolicited goods which may be left at house or delivered there. Relieves person of liability for charges for unauthorised directory entries. Prohibits unrequested distribution of advertisements for sex products. The object of the Acts is to deter those who supply unwanted goods and create a feeling of obligation to pay for them. Method known as inertia selling.

unsolicited home visits. Under the BCAP unsolicited calls should not be made on those who reply to advertisements. An adequate opportunity should be given to refuse a representative's visit. Coupons are best worded so that an enquirer can state whether or not a follow-up call is welcomed. To ask for an enquirer to state his telephone number is tantamount to inviting a follow-up phone call. *See* SALES LEAD.

upper case. Capital letters. *See* LOWER CASE.

Uppie. Unpretentious, privately individualistic egoist. *See* PSYCHOGRAPHIC TYPES.

UV varnishing. Application of varnish to covers of brochures, or emphasise certain areas of print such as illustrations.

V

valence. Aspects, such as colour and brightness, which attract or repel, so that they can be said to have positive or negative valence.

validity check. Checking of 10% or more of marketing research work every week to reduce bias and misreporting.

value. Lightness or darkness of tone of picture.

vandal proof. Protection of posters against damage by vandals, especially by printing posters (such as 4-sheets for shopping precincts) on vandal-proof material.

variable space. Spacing inserted between words to justify line and achieve an even right-hand edge.

variety, law of. In design, avoidance of monotony by use of variety of elements such as variations in typography, use of illustrations and colour.

Variojet 2800. INK JET personalisation system developed for direct mail shots and used exclusively by Colourgraphic Group, Leicester.

variometer. Instrument for measuring visual impact of an advertisement by varying amount of light available to view test subjects. Illumination is gradually increased to reveal more of the test elements. The aim is to show which elements are more legible at low level of illumination. Also called shadow box.

VCR. *See* VIDEOCASSETTE RECORDER.

VDU. *See* VISUAL DISPLAY UNIT.

vehicle. In an ink, liquid component containing the pigment.

vehicular visibility. In estimating OSCAR poster audiences, questionnaire requirements regarding deflection, obstruction, competition and distance affecting members of the travelling public. Each poster panel scored on three factors added together: visibility range, competition and angle. The resulting index is multiplied in turn by score for deflection, obstruction, height from the ground and illumination. Values for these factors by panel sizes are then set out in tables.

Verified Free Distribution. Method of assessing the distribution figure of a free newspaper. VFD figures are issued by Verified Free Distributions, a subsidiary of the Audit Bureau of Circulations, set up in 1981 to certify circulation figures of free newspapers. Delivered door-to-door with saturation coverage of urban areas, they have become an important local press advertising medium.

verso. Left-hand page, or back of a page in a book.

vertical advertising. Co-operative advertising, supplier helping distributor by various means: e.g. listing stockists in ads; supplying artwork and camera-ready copy; or contributing to cost of retailer's advertising.

vertical trade journals. Those read by people of varying status from operators to top management in the same industry, e.g. *Electronics Weekly*. *See* HORIZONTAL JOURNALS.

video paint systems. Various methods used for TV and video creative work. Systems include BBC's Flair, Apple Computers Macpaint, Quantel Paintbox, Artron, Image, Artist and Dicomed Imaginator. Alternatives to CAD/CAM systems of design computer.

video vampire. Any visual element which detracts from selling thrust of TV commercial (Rosser Reeves).

videocassette. Videotape recording contained in a cassette for playing on a VCR connected to a TV set. VHS is most popular but also on Betamax and Sony Umatic commercial format. Blank tapes for recording off-air. (*See* TIME-SHIFT BROADCASTS). Largely replaced films, but films can be transferred to video, as can slides. By means of post-production techniques many computer graphics effects can be introduced. Used for documentaries, house magazines, etc. More portable than cans of film. Can also be shown on larger screens, e.g. at conferences. Costs about £2,000-£2,500 per minute to produce.

videocassette recorder. Playback device for both recording on blank tape and for playing pre-recorded tapes via connection with TV set. *See* VIDEOCASSETTE.

videotape. Magnetic tape counterpart of sound film. In various widths for commercial/domestic, reel-to-reel and cassette formats. Most TV programmes, TV commercials and documentaries now on videotape. Computer graphics special effects can be applied.

videotext. Generic name for all VIEWDATA and teletext information systems displayed as pages on TV screens. *See* ORACLE, PRESTEL.

Viewdata. *See* PRESTEL.

viewer response service. Most TV companies offer telephone service so that viewers may respond to commercials and request literature. Can also be linked with couponed advertisements in *TV Times* and newspapers.

viewing pattern. Time of day when certain viewers watch programmes. TV commercials can be targeted accordingly.

vinyl. Removable self-adhesive vinyl used for bus advertising, especially for external positions. London Transport Advertising recommend certain makes and qualities. Preferred to paper posters which fade and saturate.

VIPS formula. David Bernstein's formula for an effective advertisement. Visibility, Identity, Promise, Singlemindedness. The advertisement should be seen, there should be no doubt about whose advertisement it is or its subject, a benefit should be offered, and the ad should stick to the point.

visual. Rough, SCAMP or scribble. Rough LAYOUT of an advertisement.

Visual Display Unit. Resembling a TV set, the monitor which gives visual presentation of computerised or keyed information.

visualiser. Artist who expresses advertisement and print ideas in rough visual form.

voice-over. Commentary by unseen speaker on film or video as often occurs with presenter on TV commercial.

volume discount. In TV airtime buying, discount to agency on large expenditures, but volume and discount varies from one TV company to another.

voucher copy. Free copy of publication containing advertisement, sent to agency or advertiser. The agency voucher clerk checks insertions, positions, colour and reproduction quality before payment is made.

W

wait order. Paper set advertisement, usually for insertion in local newspaper, awaiting advertiser's instruction to print it.

wallpaper. Way of pre-printing full-colour whole-page advertisements for black and white newspapers, using PHOTO-GRAVURE, and printing on a WEB without a break. When the web is fed into the newspaper press it is cut irrespective of match. Generally replaced by litho-printed pre-printed colour pages, or colour is printed on the run.

warm colours. Red and yellow shades, which also appear to advance whereas pale or cold colours like blue and mauve tend to recede.

Warren's Shoe Blacking. World's first product to be advertised nationally in England. Early 19th century.

wash drawing. Drawing painted in grey and black.

watermark. Made-by-wire design during papermaking, and impressed by dandy roll, to produce papermaker's trade mark or to distinguish a particular paper.

wave posting. In outdoor advertising, and especially when local promotions are being held, concentration of poster showings in a succession of areas.

wealthy empty-nesters. High income couples whose children have left home.

wear-out. Exhaustion factor which may occur in marketing research when respondents are weary of answering questions, lose interest or find test irrelevant.

weasel words. Imprecise words which evade definite statements, e.g. maybe for yes, seldom for never, not bad for good. Words which avoid admitting too much.

web. Reel of paper, or other material, used when printing by rotary press.

web-fed. Printing from web or reel of paper instead of sheets.

web-offset-litho. Rotary lithographic printing process, plate cylinder first printing onto blanket which offsets onto paper, and using webs or reels of paper instead of flat sheets. High-speed process as used for most newspaper printing.

weight. 1. The lightness or boldness of a typeface, e.g. light, medium, bold, extra bold. 2. Volume of advertising.

weight of viewing. Division of ITV audiences into heavy, light and regular viewers, approximately one third each.

weightings. In marketing research, adjustment of figures to overcome imbalance.

Welsh Fourth Channel Authority. Responsible for programme service of S4C.

wet-on-wet. Printing colours in sequence before drying, which can cause loss of REGISTER if paper stretches. Wet printing.

wf. Wrong fount. Proof reader's mark if a wrong type fount has been set.

whannies. Semi-acronym for PSYCHOGRAPHIC TYPE, we have a nanny.

White Book, The. International Production Directory of performers, services and facilities associated with the music industry, film, TV and video, concerts, shows, special events, conferences and exhibitions. The White Book, Staines, Middlesex. 1983, Annual.

white collar, white blouse workers. The social grade C^1, lower middle class such as office staff.

white line. Spacing between lines of typesetting, formerly known as leading when strips of non-type high metal were inserted between lines of metal type.

white mail. Correspondence incurred in DIRECT RESPONSE marketing due to goods out-of-stock, claims for refunds, returned goods, complaints. Some white mail can be overcome if a customer is asked to state second choice.

white out. Reverse out or printing white on another colour.

WHSTV. *See* SMITH TELEVISION, W. H.

wicketed polythene envelopes. *See* POLYTHENE ENVELOPES.

widow. Single word on last line of paragraph. Should not appear at top of a column or page. Text should be edited to eliminate widow.

window. In litho film, space where halftones are to be stripped in.

wipe. *See* OPTICALS.

wire stand. POINT-OF-SALE display piece for counter or floor. Should have a plate identifying the supplier. Very convenient display piece which retailers can abuse by using for rival products.

wire stitching. *See* SADDLE-STITCHED.

wish book. Giant MAIL ORDER catalogue, now largely replaced by small, specialist catalogues targeted at segmented markets.

wood free. Paper made of wood pulp or chemical pulp, and free from mechanical pulp, which has been cooked to dissolve lignin which otherwise causes browning effect. Better quality than NEWSPRINT. Typical white papers that stay white are coated wood free and wood free opaques.

woopies. Acronym for PSYCHOGRAPHIC GROUP 'well off older people' (over 55s). Pre-retirement market. Larger than BABY BOOMER market. Also called 'wooffies'.

word association test. Marketing research technique which requires a respondent to state words, objects, feelings, associated with given word, e.g. bread and butter, chicken and egg, hat and coat.

word break. Division of word at the end of line, which should enable word to be read easily.

work-up drawing. Preliminary sketch before finished artwork is produced.

workings. Number of times a piece of print has to pass through the machine before it is finished.

wrinklies. Elderly people, such as those who were in their 20s during Second World War. Retired people. Also called crinklies or crumblies. *See* PSYCHOGRAPHIC TYPES.

wrong fount. *See* WF.

WWAV Group Guide To Mailsort. Useful booklet explaining the operation of Post Office MAILSORT discount system. WWAV Group, London.

X, Y, Z

x-height and line. Height of small letters without ascenders or descenders, e.g. a, e, i, o, u. Letters with low x-heights are difficult to read as text type. Some display faces have low x-heights which is acceptable in large sizes, but makes type unsuitable for body matter—a fault sometimes overlooked. Also called the mean line.

xenon flash. Powerful swift light source used in photosetting.

xerography. Photocopying process in which an image is reproduced when toner adheres to paper by means of light-sensitive electrostatic charge.

xH. X-HEIGHT of lower case letters.

yapp. Edges of a binding which exceeds pages of a book, as with covers of some Bibles.

yuppie. Psychographic type young upwardly mobile professional, but originally young urban professionals. *See* PSYCHO-GRAPHIC TYPES.

Zapf Renaissance Antigua. Type family created by Herrman Zapf which contains new characters not restricted to the EM-quad, and providing unusual letterforms for advertisement setting. Supplied by Scangraphic Visutek Ltd, Leatherhead.

zapping. Flicking from one TV channel to another by use of remote control, as when viewer does not wish to watch commercials. Hazard suffered by TV advertisers unless the commercials are so compelling that zapping does not occur. Can result from a commercial being shown too frequently, especially on same day.

zipper. Special perforated seal applied to mailshots.

zoned campaigns. Advertising campaigns restricted to certain geographical areas, either to boost sales in a weak selling area, or to launch a product area by area. Regional TV stations lend themselves to this.

zoom. Using a zoom lens on a camera, to bring picture into close-up or the reverse.